My Memory is **shot**;

All I Retain Now is **water**

Marla Marton
9-2017

ALSO BY LORI BORGMAN

The Death of Common Sense and Profiles of Those Who Knew Him (2012)

Catching Christmas (2008)

All Stressed Up and No Place To Go (2005)

Pass the Faith, Please (2004)

I Was a Better Mother Before I Had Kids (1999)

MY MEMORY IS SHOT;
ALL I RETAIN NOW IS WATER

published by Good Cheer Publishing

© 2013 by Lori Borgman
International Standard Book Number:

978-1-4675-7388-7

Cover photographs
Charlie Nye

Printed in the United States of America
Country Pines Printing
Shoals, Indiana

LORI BORGMAN

My Memory is shot;
all I Retain Now is water

Introduction

ONE

A is for Atrophy

TWO

Bye Bye Birdies

Introduction

I remember holding the card in my hand and wondering if it wasn't spin. It was a note from a friend I'd known since high school. We would both be turning fifty in the coming year and her handwriting positively gushed.

> Can you believe we're turning fifty?!!
> This could be the best decade of our lives!
> Just think! There will be weddings!
> Parties! Bridal showers! And if we're lucky
> . . . maybe even grandbabies!

I was stunned. And not just by the excess of exclamation points. Weddings? Weddings are expensive. We were still recovering from the year before, when all three of our kids were in college at the same time. We were a couple for whom red meat meant raising the line on our home-equity loan.

Grandbabies? Where did that come from? I hadn't given any thought to grandbabies. It all sounded so, I don't know — old! Would grandbabies mean I should stop coloring my hair? Was it time to invest in sensible shoes? Or start buying sweaters with seasonal pictures on them? The ones with autumn leaves and pumpkins by the rail fence, or the snow-dusted cardinal in the evergreens. Like I need a calendar on my chest.

And yet, maybe it *could be* the start of wonderful things. Maybe it really *would be* a marvelous new season of life. Maybe there would be weddings! Parties! Bridal showers! And grandbabies! I resolved to be more like my friend, more open-minded to serendipitous changes around every bend. More liberal in my use of exclamation marks!!!

As it turns out, my friend was right. Let me qualify that. She was partly right. It has been a season of weddings and parties and beautiful grandbabies. Wonderful things. Marvelous things. But she was also partly wrong; it has been a season of a few other things as well.

Say hello to colonoscopies, bone density scans and frequent cholesterol checks. Jamie Lee Curtis and Activia are your new best friends. Betty White doesn't look so old anymore. Packing for a trip becomes a bigger deal. Chances are, you are now a person who "travels with meds." You and your friends have new topics of conversation, many of which include reconstructive breast surgery, hysterectomies and prostates.

It is a season when you find yourself standing in front of the bathroom mirror with your hands pulling up your forehead to envision what a brow lift might do for you.

It is the season of slower metabolism. You smell garlic and gain two pounds. I now tell every woman under forty that I meet to have a doughnut. Have two, I say, because when you hit fifty, you won't be having any.

Memory? Fuggedaboudit.

This has also been a season of grief and loss. Our parents have all died and now strangers are living in our childhood homes. We have closed the door on another generation. It is on those days in particular, when some small thing has once again triggered a flood of tears over a loved one lost, that I fantasize about going to my friend, vigorously shaking her and yelling, *"What's the matter with you? Were you nuts? This is awful!"*

No season of life is all good or all bad. There's no such thing as a best season. Every season has its potholes.

As for my friend, I should have known she was a little out of touch. After all, who writes note cards anymore?

Txt me.

1

A IS FOR ATROPHY

A Distant Memory

I don't know when it happened, or how it happened, but my memory is shot. All I retain now is water. Were it not for word association, I would not survive. Last week I was trying to think of the name of the beautiful towering trees that make Oregon so gorgeous and pristine. We lived in Oregon for nine years. Forgetting the name of those trees is like forgetting my own phone number, which I often have to say aloud several times to determine whether it starts with 833 or 873.

If I can just find a starting point, I know I can solve the puzzle. Sort of like Sudoku, or the crossword.

Pine? Were they pine? No, they weren't pine.

Scotch? No, they weren't drinking trees.

I remembered that they were well-dressed trees. I knew

I was getting warm. Literally. Down, fleece, fur. That's it — fir! Fir trees!

But what kind of fir? It is a two-part name. I could see the trees towering in the clouds, swaying in the wind, and dripping sap all over our cars. Suddenly, all I could think of was the small farm town where my mother lived as a little girl. What was the name of that town? Douglas. That's it! Douglas fir trees!

Such small feats have become exhausting. Remembering things is like playing seven degrees of separation with my brain. Or is it six degrees of separation?

Names are the worst.

It's not that I can't remember them: I can — but often not until hours later.

I loathe Kohl's. Every time I walk through their doors, I see someone I know. Not someone I can name necessarily, but someone I know.

"Hi there! How are you?" *I know you. I know that I know you; I just can't remember how I know you.*

I run through the possibilities: *You're somebody's mother, right? Did our boys play soccer together? Are you one of my former college students? You don't look mad, so I don't think so. Do I know you from church? Yes, I think we sit behind you. If I could just see the back of your head. Do I know you from the neighborhood? Are you that friend of a friend I met at a fundraiser last week?*

The last time I ran into someone I knew but couldn't remember how I knew, I could remember the woman's first name, but not her last name. I knew it had something to do with windows. Sash? Sill? Double-hung? Single-hung?

Horizontal? Sliding? Window pane? Payne! No, that wasn't it. I shot straight up in bed at 2 a.m. and yelled, "ANDERSEN!" Her last name is Andersen!

As a friend says about herself, "I have a mind like a sieve."

Being a compulsive list maker helps with remembering things, providing I can remember where I put the list. No doubt it is with my car keys, cell phone, and glasses.

Because my reading glasses (an accessory you acquire around age forty), have a long history of playing hide-and-seek, I keep a pair upstairs and a pair downstairs. When I can't find the downstairs pair, I put on the glasses that I allow myself to remove from my purse only if the downstairs pair has gone missing and I'm too lazy to walk upstairs.

Wearing my purse glasses, I told the husband that I could not find my downstairs glasses.

He looked at me like he was waiting for the punch-line. "They're on the top of your head," he finally said. "You have two pairs on top of your head." I thought my head felt a little crowded, and it sure wasn't from memory cells.

Spanx Spoken Here

Some women wonder how they will know when they are on the downhill slide. I can tell you exactly how you will know. It's when you wake up one morning and your skin no longer fits. That may sound funny to you pretty young things with the twenty-two-inch waists, but that's only because you haven't lived it yet. Trust me; twenty years from now, you won't be laughing.

A friend says that she weighed the exact same weight at fifty that she did when she was twenty. "I'm the same weight I've always been," she says, "but it's all shifted."

Of course it has shifted. Nothing is where it used to be. For everything to be where it used to be, most of us would have to walk on our hands.

Knowing how to age well is important. It is an art

really, and becoming a lost art at that. I honestly believe that my grandmother's generation may have been the last group of women to age naturally. Rarely did they hit bottom because of wrinkles and the relentless pull of gravity. If they escaped bursitis and gout, they were happy campers.

When they became grandmothers, they let their hair go gray, strapped on an apron, laced up a pair of sturdy shoes, and went to the kitchen to begin baking cookies.

Today's grandmas don't do that. Today's grandmas are getting Botox injections, wearing stilettos and going on cruises to Hawaii with their live-in boyfriends. Today's grandmas do not bake cookies; they send gift cards from Pottery Barn. Women today age differently. Reluctantly. Begrudgingly. If surgically possible, not at all — I give you Joan Rivers and Cher.

We are the generation of moisturizers, wrinkle erasers, and firming lotions guaranteed to firm skin that wasn't firm twenty years ago.

And now it turns out, most of us have been focused on our faces when we should have been focused on our arms. This is according to a highly excitable woman on one of those home shopping programs.

Under different circumstances, I might find Rhonda somewhat heroic, because few women I know would extend their arms before a television camera and jiggle the flab hanging beneath, while screaming and writhing in disgust at their own bodies. Rhonda said the answer to this horror is something called — ready? — the Arm Shaper.

The Arm Shaper looks like a stretch of panty hose someone pulled over his head and then threw out of a car window after knocking off a convenience store. But, as Rhonda demonstrated, the Arm Shaper does not go over the head; it goes over the arm, like a long tube sock without a toe in it. Rhonda slipped an Arm Shaper on one arm and then the other. Voila! Her arms no longer jiggled. I'm sure this was a relief to viewers everywhere, although those watching with me simply said, "Ewwwwww!"

Despite a fascinating presentation, Rhonda failed to address the matter of what wearers of the Arm Shaper might say when asked, "So, what's with the panty hose on your arm?"

But now Rhonda came to her final selling point. The Arm Shaper could take care of another awful, ugly, unsightly, extremely disgusting phenomenon women must confront — the elbow. Yes, ladies, forget your face, your weight, your backside, your front side. Your elbows may be the most hideous, revolting sign of age.

Wonder why you didn't get the big promotion?

Elbows, honey, elbows!

Turned down for a second mortgage?

Well, what did you think with elbows like those?

And don't you just know what all those young guys

are saying when pretty girls walk by: "Whoa! Get a load of those elbows!"

Here's an example of a woman aging better than most: Joan Collins. Ms. Collins is the actress who was on the evening soap "Dynasty" years ago. She looks good for her age. Maybe you heard about what happened to her. Ms. Collins wore a dress so tight at an Oscar party that it made her pass out. I found a picture of the dress online. It was a pretty dress, and not just pretty tight. She looked like a beautiful purple mermaid covered in jewels, pushing up two coconuts from the deep plunging neckline.

Joan Collins was seventy-seven at the time. Old enough to start thinking about veiling the coconuts and hiking up the neckline, but like a lot of women, she may have some issues with dressing her age.

Collins said the dress was so constricting it made her feel dizzy; then she fainted in the arms of her husband — who is thirty-two years her junior. When she came to, she was surrounded by handsome firemen.

And for this we should feel sorry?

My personal hunch is that it wasn't just the tight dress that made Collins swoon; it may have been the undergarment beneath the dress. The entire fiasco has Spanx written all over it. For those of you not abreast of ladies' shapewear, a Spanx is a small tube of industrial strength Spandex strong enough to catapult a space shuttle to Mars. A woman squeezing herself into a Spanx is similar to a Polar bear squeezing itself through the PVC pipe beneath your kitchen sink.

I was the first to advocate that Spanx come with a caution from the Surgeon General: "Warning: Spanx may cause shortness of breath, light-headedness, heartburn, and the feeling that you are being sliced in two directly beneath the rib cage."

My first and last tangle with a Spanx was when I purchased a special occasion dress for a black-tie event. The alterations lady said the dress was a lovely fit, but the sales clerk said I might like to try a Spanx for extra support. If the Supreme Court has any lingering doubts as to what obscenity is, it is a fifty-something woman squeezing herself into a Spanx.

"Just step into it and shake yourself down," the clerk said. She then proceeded to wait outside the fitting room. Apparently I wasn't shaking it down fast enough, as she began shouting, "Work it, girl, work it!" I was mortified. I considered not leaving the fitting room until after the store had closed.

Unfortunately, I didn't know then what I know now. And I'm thinking Joan Collins will thank me for knowing about this, too — Pajama Jeans. Maybe you've seen the commercials: "That's right — looks like denim, feels like PJs!"

The television commercial says Pajama Jeans are ideal for exercise, travel, shopping, "and more." I think the "and more" is Thanksgiving dinner, Christmas dinner, barbecue, bakery goods, loaded baked potatoes, and three-cheese nachos. "And more" might even mean sleeping in them and wearing them again the next day.

There is no shaking or "working it girl" to get into Pajama Jeans. Pajama Jeans are forgiving, so forgiving that you probably won't even notice that you have been eating, sleeping, and lounging in them for weeks at a time, gaining forty pounds without a moment of discomfort.

The best part is, you will never pass out or lose consciousness in Pajama Jeans. Of course, that also means you just lost your chance of coming to surrounded by attractive firemen.

Sticking Your Neck Out

A young woman was on one of those plastic surgery shows complaining that her perky parts weren't perky enough, her thin parts weren't thin enough, and her curvy parts weren't curvy enough. She looked to be thirty which made her only slightly less annoying than the twenty-some-things doing commercials for moisturizers. "Used nightly, this miracle moisturizer will take ten years off your face!" This would make the model age eleven. Please.

I looked at the gal on screen and thought, "Sweetie, the first thing you could do to improve your looks is chip off some of that makeup, give up the booze, and get a good night's sleep." And I wonder why they never ask me to produce.

In any case, the doctor was nodding and offering a sincere "hmmm" to all of her concerns. Then, in a voice-over, the doctor said he was going to make this young woman perkier, firmer, curvier, and, "give her the most popular surgery package in California today by also giving her a Brazilian butt."

I knew that as women we were supposed to be relentlessly critical of our faces, our arm flab, and our belly fat, but I had no idea we had agreed to turn on our backsides as well. Let the record note that I disagree with the decision to turn on our backsides.

The front side is where it is happening, which is why women, particularly aging women, always focus on accessories like chunky bracelets, big necklaces, and oversized handbags. It makes sense. If we can get someone to notice our accessories, they are less likely to notice our crow's feet, the little pouches under our eyes, or that little tuft of cheek positioning itself to become a full-fledged jowl.

Scarves have been the go-to accessories for several seasons now. I'd accessorize with a scarf every day of the week, except I'm missing one critical element — the neck of a giraffe.

I am a member of the short-neck group. I never thought of my neck as short until I wrapped a silk scarf around it three times, exactly the way I saw it done on a mannequin. The mannequin looked sleek and sophisticated. I look like someone pounded my head into my chest.

If I'd had a top hat and a carrot nose, I could have

passed for a snowman.

I should have known. The mannequin had an eighteen-inch neck and a reed-thin, pasty-white body made entirely of lightweight plastic. I birthed babies that weighed more.

Every year, fashion incites women to turn on yet another body part. Hemlines rise and women curse pudgy knees. Hemlines fall to mid-calf and another subset of women detest their piano legs and thick ankles. The sleeve-less returns and women despise their arms with a vengeance.

Yet, in the spirit of "can do," I try another scarf, tying it in a fashionable manner. I look like a flight attendant. *Soft drink, coffee, juice?*

I try it again with a slightly different flair. I look like a political protestor waiting for the release of tear gas.

I read a pamphlet titled "Eight Ways to Tie a Scarf" explaining how I might achieve a variety of cosmopolitan looks. The instructions seem vaguely familiar. I've seen them before somewhere. It was in the knot-tying section of the Boy Scout Handbook.

I attempt the muffler, looping both ends of the scarf around the back of my neck, crossing sides, bringing them forward and tucking them under. Great. I look like I am wearing a bib. I look stuffed, like I ate too much for dinner and am totally miserable. They should market this with an antacid.

And, I ask, what do you do with scarves with the

really long tails? Let them hang? What if they don't hang straight down? What if they go over a slight rise on their way down and they swing? What is the proper scarf tail etiquette? Do you hold them down when you walk, or do you let the tails gain momentum and lash passersby? I don't think we have insurance for that.

Dramatic types intuitively know what to do with long scarves. They casually give one end a flick over the shoulder. They wave the scarf as they tell stories and laugh. I would try these things, laughing and waving my scarf in a Diane Keaton and Meryl Streep sort of way, but I would not be able to pull it off. Friends would quietly suggest that I consider medication.

A first cousin to the scarf, but one that requires absolutely no tying, is the poncho. A poncho is a tablecloth with a hole in the middle for your head. It wraps around you like a warm blanket and covers every single body flaw from the neck to the knees. The poncho is fashion's gift to post-menopausal women.

I've also noticed that every picture of a woman wearing a poncho shows the woman walking into the wind. I gather that the trick to getting all that fabric to stay in place is to lean into the wind. I can meet you for lunch in my trendy poncho, but only on windy days.

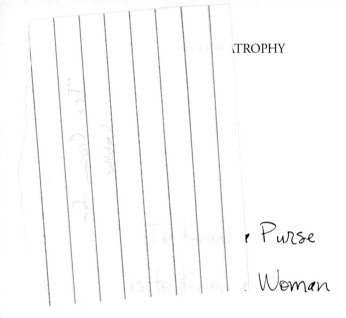

Purse Woman

I have long contended that you can tell what stage of life a woman is in by the purse she carries. A female who carries one of those tiny purses no bigger than a slice of bread is packing nothing more than one lip gloss, a tube of mascara, a driver's license, and a major credit card. This woman is usually very young, very rich, and very thin. I don't like her.

Women who carry mid-sized shoulder bags are light years beyond that minimalist thing. They are packing coupon folders, bills to be mailed, and bundles of punch cards (buy twelve loaves of bread and get a loaf free). This is the purse of a survivalist. This is a woman with children. She is the designated packhorse for the entire family, be it trips to the library or vacations to the Smoky Mountains. Her purse warehouses sunblock, stamps for postcards, manicure supplies, anti-bacterial hand gel, saltines wrapped in cellophane, and dried fruit snacks. This is the woman and purse to approach in case of hunger or medical emergency.

A woman with an enormous purse resembling a backpack or bowling bag is one of three types. She is a young mother with a baby, packing diapers, towelettes, teething gel, chubby books, strained carrots, and plastic play toys; she is a woman to whom the phrase "travel light" has absolutely no meaning; or she is a grandmother who needs extra space in her purse for all those 8 x 10s of the grandchildren.

We women take pride in our purses. Dare I say we can be a tad competitive? Last week someone mentioned they had a headache and I found myself in the middle of another purse war.

I reached in my bag and pulled out Tylenol just as another woman reached in her bag and pulled out Extra Strength Tylenol, Arthritis Strength Tylenol, and gel Tylenol.

She threw them down like she just played a royal flush.

I dove back into my bag, suggested the woman with the headache consider ibuprofen, and threw down a travel-size bottle of Motrin.

Take that you oversized orange pleather job with the big silver buckle.

Whereupon, Big Orange pulled out sample packets of both Excedrin and Midol, tossed them to the woman now holding her head in her hands, and told her to keep her options open.

We women often open our handbags looking like we're Good Samaritans, but deep down, we know it's really a contest to find out who has the best stocked purse.

Someone sneezes and the race is on. A metallic clutch yields a dainty pink travel pack of tissues. A big brown shoulder bag produces a full-size designer box of Kleenex and announces they have lanolin for sensitive skin.

Some purses can be so haughty.

If you really want to see the purse wars heat up, spill something on your clothes. I recently saw a man spill coffee on his white shirt. He was instantly assaulted by one woman with a Shout Wipe, two women with Tide To Go stain remover pens, and another with an OxiClean pen. The shirt came clean, but the man was permanently traumatized.

A well-packed purse should be able to do hair and makeup on the spot, replenish school supplies, and treat superficial wounds.

I once attended a luncheon where women won prizes for having the most bizarre items in their handbags. The winner was a mother of three children under the age of four. She produced a pair of Scooby Doo underwear, a pair of Barbie underwear, training pants for her toddler, and a pair of underpants for herself. As she ripped them out of her purse and waved them over her head, the entire room fell silent.

A few seconds passed and then we all offered up a round of applause. We women may be competitive, but we know a well-stocked purse when we see it.

The Gym and I

I go to a gym. I don't go to stay fit; I go so that I can continue to eat. Your metabolism slows as you age and then one day it simply dies. That is the same day that food goes from being a pleasure to an *ought*. You *ought* to have more fiber. You *ought* to have more protein. You *ought* to have more vegetables. You *ought* to have it poached. You *ought* to have low-fat. You *ought* to have soy. You *ought* to work out.

So I joined a gym. It was one of those franchise gyms that has a little television attached to each and every treadmill and cross trainer. When I joined the gym, they had the Food Network. You could pound your heart out while watching Giada De Laurentiis mix up a three-cheese rigatoni with enough fat grams to take you through the middle of next week.

I found myself timing my visit to the gym around the

Food Network lineup. I am not proud of this. In fact, I tried to be somewhat secretive. I would manage to get a machine on the back row where no one could see what I watched. That way I could hold my head up while I worked out and simultaneously watch Ina Garten pile a chocolate mousse into a pastry shell.

If someone got on the treadmill next to me, I'd switch to cable news so I didn't look like a total slacker. The Food Network began motivating me to work out.

And then the Food Network disappeared. At first, I thought maybe the machine I was on wasn't getting good satellite reception; so I moved to the machine next to it. And to the next one and to the next one. There are only so many machines you can move to before you begin drawing attention to yourself.

I was pretty sure they discontinued the Food Network. I was crestfallen.

What was I supposed to do? Sashay up to one of the ultra-thin, ultra-fit, "I-hate-fat" trainers and demand they bring back the Food Network? Like they care that I can't watch Paula Deen lower fritters into a bubbling vat of melted fat.

These trainers were fit. They were so lean that even their names were thin: Ki, Rys, Su.

I could mention the situation to the front desk, but I worried the next time I checked in someone would get on the loud speaker and say, "She's here — the woman who vicariously consumes more calories than she burns during each and every workout. Please join us in making her feel bloated."

I considered dropping a note in the suggestion box, but they had surveillance cameras.

It's not like I was asking them to install vending machines with Cheetos or Hagen Dazs. I just wanted something besides news and sports to watch on the tube.

I eventually left the gym for a cheaper gym, but not nearly in the grand fashion that a friend did.

She, too, was going to the gym until she fell off the wagon, or the treadmill rather. She worked with a trainer for nine weeks and walked her rear end off on the treadmill. Diligently. Faithfully.

Her trainer was a young guy, real nice. She got to know him like a son — where his family was from, where he was going on vacation. She sweat and ached and did everything he told her to do. She didn't get dramatic results, but she was grateful.

On her last day, to show her thanks, she made caramel corn for the front desk and baked the trainer a blueberry pie.

Do These Scales Make Me Look Thin?

At eight o'clock one night our son-in-law stepped on a scale to weigh himself. He had just eaten a full meal. He was fully clothed, with pants, shirt, heavy shoes, a belt, and was holding one of his nine-month-old twins.

He stepped on the scale, waited for it to register, stepped off, and announced his weight to the room.

"A woman would never do that," I said to my daughter.

"Certainly not," she answered.

A woman doesn't broadcast the weight a scale gives her because a woman doesn't accept the weight a scale gives her.

Women argue with scales.

Is this thing on an incline or what?

It was that ham sandwich; ham makes me retain water.

I wonder if I have that disorder where people crawl out of bed and eat in the night?

It's all these hair products weighing me down.

A woman weighs herself in the morning, not the evening.

A woman weighs herself before she eats, not after.

A woman also weighs herself before she showers — water droplets add pounds.

No woman believes the scale at the doctor's office either. Every last one of them weighs heavy. It's a conspiracy that Oliver Stone should look into.

However, there was one day that I was in total agreement with the bathroom scale.

I stepped on the scale and saw the unexplained weight loss nearly every woman dreams of. I weighed fifty-seven pounds. I knew that couldn't possibly be right, so I stepped on it again.

Sure enough, fifty-seven had been a bad read. The scale said I actually weighed fifty-eight.

Technically, I should be traveling in a car seat. That's me, the one in the driver's seat of an SUV strapped in a child's car seat with tilt recline and side beverage cupholder.

The last time I weighed fifty-eight, I was probably in the fourth grade. I knew all my states and capitals then. I loved converting fractions, wrote a poem once a week, was the jump rope champion, had legible handwriting, and enjoyed recess twice a day. My mother did my laundry and cooked all the meals and I could still overpower my younger brother. It was a good year, one I wouldn't mind revisiting.

It was nice to weigh fifty-eight again. It made me feel light, inside and out. My clothes fit better. My jeans felt loose. I felt healthier. More energetic. More vibrant. Maybe I'd swim a couple hundred meters. I've never been a swimmer, but why should that stop me?

Yes, it did occur to me that the digital scale was on the fritz, but I immediately put that thought out of my mind. Why let common sense ruin a wonderful start to a beautiful day?

We went out to lunch later and I had biscuits. I don't eat biscuits. I don't even like biscuits, but when you have unexpected weight loss, you feel entitled to eat biscuits.

Pass the butter.

I had ice cream, too. Not much, but a little. It's been months since I had ice cream. It's on my banned food list. But I was eating ice cream now.

As I poured a little chocolate syrup on my ice cream, I wondered if I should call the doctor so he could update my medical records. Maybe my cholesterol numbers had taken a dramatic dive, too.

Later that night the husband walked to the 'fridge,

opened the door, and casually said, "I weighed seventy-five pounds this morning."

"Really?" I asked. "I only weighed fifty-eight. You should go on a diet."

We ordered pizza.

Life was good for a few days. We ate what we wanted, pretended we were both grossly underweight, and then it all came to a crashing halt.

We bought a new scale.

Dreaming of a Good Night's Sleep

Been sleeping like a baby lately — a baby that wakes up at midnight and doesn't go back to sleep until three.

Do you watch the clock, or not watch the clock? Recite passages from memory or say the alphabet backward?

It's dark. I can barely make out the shape of the old secretary (a piece of furniture, not a woman) sitting in our bedroom. A side view of the piece resembles the profile of Abraham Lincoln. Wonder what Lincoln's doing?

The furnace just kicked in again. Round nine.

This is how people get started listening to talk radio at night.

I wonder if I can name all the Supreme Court justices. Yep, I can name all ten. (That was a joke.)

How can he sleep like that? My pillow has gone flat.

Is that moonlight hitting the blinds? Wonder what phase the moon is in? Maybe I should look. No, I heard when you can't sleep, it's better to lie still, because a body at rest recharges more than a body in motion.

If I did check on the moon, I could get some ice cream while I'm up. I heard a spoonful of ice cream can help you sleep. I'm willing to try. I'll probably get all the way downstairs to the freezer and find all we have are frozen chicken breasts. Those could help you sleep — if you smacked yourself on the head with them. I'm almost willing to try.

I should organize the linen closet tomorrow.

Was that a door? None of our neighbors are out this late. Could be the leaning tower of Tupperware on that closet shelf shifting again.

Maybe it was an intruder. If it is an intruder, he's quiet now. Probably listening for footsteps. He's not going to hear my footsteps, until I hear his footsteps. Two can play this game, buddy.

The last time I heard an intruder, it was the hot water heater. The time before that . . . well, there's no point in dredging up the past. Who has time? Time, time, time.

If it really is an intruder, we should have an exit plan.

I'll need the sheets. I can tie them together, tether one end to the legs of the wingback chair and we can lower ourselves out the window. I could be over reacting, but what if I'm not?

If I could just roll him over. I've seen nurses change sheets with patients still in the bed. Wish I'd paid closer attention. Ugh. There we go. I need to move his legs. How can legs . . . be . . . so . . . heavy?

Once I knot the sheets, they'll lose length. I may need the window coverings as well.

Funny, I haven't heard anything from the intruder. Hmmm.

Oh, great. Now the husband is stirring. If I hold still and freeze — which I already am without sheets and a blanket — maybe he won't wake up.

"Why is it so cold?" he mutters, without opening his eyes.

"You probably heard me say I was going for ice cream. Go back to sleep."

If there is an intruder, maybe he'd like some ice cream. The night is young. I hope he'll stay and talk.

The Doctor Is In

Once you hit fifty, you should start looking around for health care professionals who are considerably younger than you are. You want your doctor to outlive you. When our doctor retired, he referred his patients to a young man just setting up practice. It was wonderful. He only had a few patients and we had no problem getting in to see him. Then other people started turning fifty, thinking they, too, should find a younger doctor and, consequently, it is now nearly impossible to get an appointment.

Having realized that the key to getting an appointment with my doctor is to pre-plan illnesses and injuries at least six weeks in advance, I switched doctors. I now doctor with Dr. Nancy Snyderman on NBC-TV's "Today Show."

She keeps morning hours and, best of all, I don't have to go to her — she comes to me. Of course, that's provid-

ing I remember to turn on the television. And release the mute.

You're wondering what if the problems Dr. Snyderman is talking about aren't the problems I have, right? Originally, I thought that might be a problem, too. But having been blessed with a vivid imagination, I find that I usually begin experiencing at least one or two symptoms of the topic she is discussing by the time her segment is finished.

I don't mean to brag, but my television doctor, Dr. Snyderman, is very knowledgeable about a lot of things — heart disease, diabetes, high blood pressure, menopause, stress, sex problems, and obesity.

She falls just short of the doctors on the cable news shows who can tell you what a high profile person is thinking, what motivates them, what drives them, even though they have never been in the same room with that person. Those doctors are obviously clairvoyant. Dr. Snyderman is good, but she is not clairvoyant.

Last week I informed the youngest that my doctor says there is no such thing as a base-line tan. "My doctor says any tan is a sign that skin has been sun-damaged," I said. The kid hangs out at her apartment complex pool a lot, so I thought I should throw a little fear into her.

"Are you quoting your doctor from the 'Today Show?'" she asks.

"Who else?" I ask. "You have a better one?"

"Yes," she snips. "'The Doctors.'"

"Isn't that the one with a bunch of doctors sitting around a table? I should have known you'd go for that talk-show format. Listen, just because it's a group of doctors doesn't necessarily mean you'll get better care.

"Sweetie, have you considered Dr. Oz? He's older and more experienced. He has a lovely bedside manner and can also conduct a large group intervention with the help of a sympathetic studio audience."

"Are you serious?" she says, peering over the top of her sunglasses. "Have you not seen Dr. Travis Stork on 'The Doctors?'"

"I haven't *seen* him, *seen* him, but I have seen a promo or two. Is he the young good looking one in scrubs?"

"Exactly," she says. "And he's also tan. Tell that to your 'Today Show' doctor. You should think about switching, Mom. 'The Doctors' also have a plastic surgeon in the roundtable."

"I'll ignore that," I said. "What do you think I am? Some willy nilly doctor shopper? Besides, I never have the television on after 9 a.m."

Thermostat-Control Leg

Another thing you can look forward to as you age is your internal thermostat blowing out. It becomes increasingly hard to get the temperature regulated just the way you like it. This is partly due to age, but it is also because your spouse invariably hovers toward the opposite end of the thermostat. Naturally, if you like the temperature on the cool side, you will marry someone who can never pile the bedding high enough, owns thermal underwear and wore socks to bed as a child.

Embracing these differences in thermostat settings and being willing to inflict your preference on your spouse is one of the unwritten mandates of marriage.

Because I have always liked being on the cool side, I often run about without a coat, instead wearing an insulated vest of some sort.

I was waiting in line to check out at a sporting goods store when a woman ahead of me said, "I like your vest." It was a quilted corduroy vest with a fake fur collar.

"Wouldn't that be perfect for running in and out of stores in the cold?" she said to her friend.

"Like sleeping with one leg out," the woman said.

I was stunned. Speechless.

Here, all this time, I thought I was the only one who regulated my internal thermostat by sleeping with one leg out.

The ladies represented an entire demographic (and one apparently now going public) that sleeps with one leg out.

If you don't know what I'm talking about, you're not one of us.

We are the sleepers who throw one leg out from beneath the covers to keep from overheating.

Some refer to it as the thermostat-control leg.

There are also variations on the theme. There is the thermostat-control arm and the thermostat-control foot for those who can regulate their internal temperature by merely venting an arm or a foot. Special kudos to those who can regulate body temperature by venting only the big toe.

Whenever I espouse my belief that it is healthier to be on the cold side rather than the warm side, particularly at night, the husband often says, "Why don't we just sleep outside?"

"Why don't we?" I chirp. "Our ancestors did."

He claims his ancestors did not sleep outside, but came from a long line of luxury hotel chain magnates that cranked the thermostat to eighty degrees in each and every room.

It is for the family's own good that I keep the thermostat set low.

When certain family members stop by, they frequently complain about the temperature in the house. We have one daughter who often refuses to remove her coat.

"My hands are frozen," she will say.

"Put them in this warm dishwater," I say. "That will fix everything."

Another one complains, "My feet are turning to ice."

"Well, of course they are," I say. "You need to keep moving. Why don't you run this laundry upstairs? Then you can sweep the kitchen and unload the dishwasher. You'll feel warmer in no time."

It is reassuring to know that I am not alone in the one-leg-out routine in my quest for cooler air and productive living.

Maybe we'll start a support group. We can meet at my place.

Wear a jacket.

(Not So) Happy Birthday to Me

No one knows how to bleed the fun out of a birthday like the mail carrier.

My birthday is not for another few days, but the birthday greetings started arriving last week. On Tuesday, the mailman brought a postcard from the Department of Motor Vehicles telling me to enjoy my birthday, and when it was over to visit one of their branches or their website to renew my license. My driver's license won't expire until next year on my birthday, but they'd like me to save time and avoid the rush.

The postcard had a cupcake with a candle on it, so I'm trying to overlook the fact that the message was a little naggy. I've got twelve months to renew. What's the rush?

Maybe they think I won't make it another twelve

months and want their money now. Not a bad strategy in a downturn economy.

On Wednesday, I received a birthday card from a company I won't name offering to talk with me about my life insurance situation. Happy birthday to you, too.

That doesn't happen in your thirties and forties.

The real kicker was Thursday — a postcard announcing it was time for a colonoscopy. It didn't say Happy Birthday, but the timing was suspicious.

On Friday, I received an ivory envelope containing an invitation to a free dinner at one of the better steak houses in town. The husband and I could have our choice of three entrees as long as we agreed to stick around and listen to some ideas about long-term financial planning.

Apparently the colonoscopy people were miffed I didn't respond to the postcard earlier in the week, because by the end of the week they had sent a one-page letter reminding me again.

I'm so hurt. Nothing from the dentist or the OB/GYN.

All I'm missing is a card from my hairdresser suggesting it's time for color, a brochure on brow-lifts and liposuction from a plastic surgeon, and a refrigerator magnet listing the warning signs of heart attack and stroke.

Hold on, the mail just came. I now have in my hands a greeting card with a beautiful photograph of rolling emerald hills and large shade trees. Have I considered a prepaid burial?

So far the only upbeat card I've gotten is from Stein Mart. They want to give me twenty percent off any one item for my birthday. Talbots sent a birthday card, too, but they're only offering me fifteen percent off.

I started getting birthday wishes on Facebook five days before my birthday. I appreciate the kind thoughts, but I'm in no hurry. I'd like to drag this year out as long as possible before rolling over to a new number — or a new plot, if the cemetery people get their way.

I wish everyone would back off. I haven't even had a piece of cake yet. That's right, I'm having cake. Or tiramisu. Or cheesecake. Whatever it is, it will be tasty, high calorie, loaded with fat, and I will enjoy every wonderful bite.

Don't even think about it Weight Watchers, Nutrisystem, and Jenny Craig.

And for the record, I don't care what kind of downer cards I get in the mail, I plan on having another good year.

Just As I Am

You would think that when you are middle aged and then some, when your skin no longer fits, your metabolism has died, and the effects of gravity start to show, that you could go to the mall without being chased.

I was walking at a brisk clip down the center of the mall when a young man began strolling alongside me. He introduced himself as Antonio.

Antonio had smooth brown skin, jet black hair, and dark eyes. I think he was the July cover of Men's Health.

I was flattered. And then I caught a glimpse of a sign just over Antonio's shoulder. It said, "Better than Botox."

Antonio was holding a tube of something in his hand and not looking into my eyes, but around them.

"If you could just give me a moment," Antonio purred.

"They were gifts," I snap.

"But I can help you," he cajoled.

"They were gifts from my children and I like them," I said.

Antonio gave me one last look of pity and turned away.

Ten paces later, another young man approached and politely offered to fix my hair.

It was one of those days when I apparently had Fixer Upper stamped on my head.

This fellow was young, tall, lanky, and had the tips of his hair highlighted orange. He was waving a flat iron used for straightening hair, melting steel, and searing steak. He wanted to straighten and smooth some waves in my hair.

"I appreciate the offer, but this is my hair. It's frizzy, curly, wavy, and, no matter what I do, I always look like I just rolled out of bed. It took a long time, but I've learned to live with it and I think if you work at it, you can learn to live with it, too."

He looked dejected, like he might cry. I offered to get him a soft pretzel from the food court, but he shuffled back to his kiosk and slumped into his chair.

I took three more steps when Raul asked if he could weave some eighteen-inch extenders in my hair. "You'd like the look," he whispered.

"The only women my age who wear extenders are on 'Dancing With the Stars,'" I said. "My invitation was lost in the mail."

I ventured a few feet farther and a guy named Adam asked for my hand, so he could buff my nails. For a small fortune I could soften my cuticles, relax my hands, and have naturally smooth nails that reflect the sheen of track lighting.

I no sooner got my hand back from Adam when Will from Verizon wanted to switch me over from Sprint, interest me in a few apps, or at the very least persuade me to buy a jeweled case so my cell phone wouldn't look so last year.

Clutching my plain cell phone in my hand — the one with the torn cuticles and ragged fingernails — took four more steps and ran into Tom, who thought I needed a college sweatshirt with a hood. (Probably so I could pull the hood over my face.)

Two steps later, a young man named Trevor approached. I was prepared to snap his head off when he asked if I'd be interested in a lighted painting of the ocean, which features digital animation allowing the viewer to sit for hours watching the waves gently lap the shore.

I'll never forget Trevor. He is the only person at the mall who accepts me as I am.

2

BYE BYE BIRDIES

Call Me

It's not like the empty nest phase came as a shock. We didn't expect them to live at home forever. I prepared myself for when this time would come. I did some reading and talked to friends. It sounded like when your children left home, you grew depressed, moody, and cried a lot. It seemed like something to really look forward to.

My mother never indulged her emotions the way a lot of women today do. She used to say, "Empty nest syndrome nothing, we were stepping on your fingers so you'd quit holding on."

As a matter of fact, when my brother moved out, it looked more like an eviction than a move. A friend of my brother's had a truck that he used for paper routes. They had to load and unload the truck fast, as the friend was due to run another route. Mom and Dad helped pile boxes and odds and ends at the curb, including a VW bumper and an orange highway cone. "Stack it high and drive fast," my mother instructed.

For me, the Empty Nest Syndrome was short lived because it was soon eclipsed by the Heavy Breathing Syndrome. It was shortly after the kids left home that the phone calls started. There was a time when I could answer the phone, hear heavy breathing and know it was an obscene phone call. It was something I could count on — sort of like death and taxes. Today, if I answer the phone and hear heavy breathing, it is likely to be one of the kids.

"Hi, Mom — pant, huff, gasp — I'm on my way into the building. Walk me to work?"

Her breathing grows heavier and the phone is jostling so much that I can only make out every fifth word. "Saturday . . . pant, huff, puff . . . weekend . . . football . . . whoo, whoo, whoo . . . fire, flames . . . pant, gasp, pant . . . bye.

It could have been something about a Saturday football game or that her apartment caught fire. There's no way to know. Either way, it was sure nice talking to her.

If I pick up the phone and hear short little gasps with a click, click, click in the background, this would be the kid wearing dress shoes, leaving the hospital after rounding and wanting company while she walks through the parking lot.

"Nice of you to call," I say.

"Well, (wheeze, gasp, wheeze) I have a couple of minutes."

Or less. When I hear the clinking of keys and ding, ding, ding (the door chime), it means she has reached her car and the conversation is about to come to an abrupt end.

The other day I picked up the phone and heard an unfamiliar "ha, ha, ha, hee, hee, hee" breathing pattern.

"Who is this?" I demanded to know.

"It's your son."

"Well, you're scaring me because that is the breathing pattern your father and I learned for transitional labor in our Lamaze class. You're not pregnant, are you?"

"No, but — ha, ha, hee — hold on a sec."

The scream of a siren and a terrific roar blast through the phone.

"What's going on? It sounds like you're standing on a train track."

"Almost," he huffed and puffed. "That was the El at the same time a police car shot by. I'm running to the platform — ha, ha, ha, hee, hee, hee — to catch my train. I thought we could — ha, ha, ha, hee, hee, hee — talk on the way."

I'm glad they call. I just never pictured myself as running an escort service.

Yours, Mine, and Theirs

The truth is, I was never worried about losing my identity when the kids left home. There was a time, though, when I did worry about losing my mind.

The first time we visited our son's place, I remember opening a kitchen drawer and saying, "Hey, I used to have kitchen towels like this. We must have the same taste in kitchen towels. Isn't that a coincidence?"

He just smiled.

I opened a cabinet and said, "I used to have a mixing bowl like that one, too. What are the odds we'd both have the same taste in bowls?"

He avoided eye contact.

"And, look! I have measuring cups like yours, too. And hot pads!"

He said he had to walk the dog.

I realized I wasn't losing my mind; I was just losing my stuff.

When our second one left home for good, she was 600 miles away, but would often call around dinner time — to talk about meat. She is a good cook. It's just that she's never been a big red meat person and happened to marry a wonderful young man who has long hollow legs and is a serious carnivore.

Monday, 5:30 p.m. the phone rings: "Mom? What's a skirt steak?"

"I'm not sure," I say.

"I'm making fajitas and the recipe calls for skirt steak. Can't you at least take a guess? Please?"

"Fine," I say. "I'd guess a skirt steak is a steak that would look good with a sweater set and pair of boots."

Clever word play is not appreciated at a time of culinary crisis.

Thursday, 6:05: "Hey, Mom. What does flank steak look like?"

I wonder if she thinks I redecorated since she left and have a poster above my computer of a steer with dotted lines across its naked body, indicating the cuts of meat?

"Flank steak is the steak that moves in after the front lines have advanced. Honey, you're the one that married military; you ought to know this stuff."

Friday, 6:30: "Mom? I'm going to make Swiss steak in the slow cooker over the weekend and need round steak."

Great. I can see it in my head. She is now shopping for meat by shape. Round steak, cube steak, it all makes perfect sense, doesn't it?

"Mom? I found round, but it's bottom round and the recipe says top round. Do you think it will do?"

"Honey, you just take that bottom round, flip it over, and you've got your top round."

"Great!" she says.

"You're welcome, dear. May the beef be with you."

When the last one left home, we were pros at boxing, packing, and saying goodbye.

"Take anything you might need to set up housekeeping," I said. "Take anything at all."

Three days after she was gone, I discovered nearly all the DVDs were missing.

I was thinking she would take things along the lines of laundry detergent or cleaning supplies. Maybe she'd take a few staples, say a box of crackers, and a jar of peanut butter. What did I know? I wasn't twenty-three.

It's not like she bears sole responsibility for our dwindling inventory. When her older brother left, he cleaned out all the action flicks, nature shows, guided tours of hunting deer, and calling wild turkeys. When he took his haul, we welcomed the extra storage space.

The girls took the romantic comedies. That was OK, too. How many times do you want to watch the "Runaway Bride" run?

The kids claim they took the DVDs because they were the ones who bought them. Maybe so, but we were the ones who housed the DVDs, ejected them from the DVD player, and lovingly put them back in their covers at night.

In any case, our DVD supply is what you'd call slim pickins. They did leave a few. We still have "10-Minute Pilate Solutions" and "Tae-Bo: the Basic Workout with Billy Blanks." Such thoughtful children to consider their parents' health.

They also left us with a good supply of aging VHS tapes. Thank goodness we still have "Heidi," "Freaky Friday," "Parent Trap," "Beauty and the Beast," and "Aladdin." It's the Grade School Collection.

"Honey, what would you like to watch tonight? Lindsay Lohan before she hit the skids or Shirley Temple winding through the Alps?"

Good news. The husband was rustling through the remains in the cabinet, and found one they missed. "We have 'The Matrix,'" he said.

"Let's lock the doors," I told the husband, "and screen our calls."

To Ninety

When your kids spread out, it is a challenge to find ways to spend time with them. When you do find a way to spend time with one of them, it is always a shame when you wind up yelling.

On one such excursion, our oldest daughter and I were in the western suburbs of Chicago with the intention of reaching downtown at rush hour. It was just the two of us, with a chance to have some good conversation and catch up on life.

However, if we had entered this trip into Mapquest, it would have returned a page with driving instructions that said: Stay where you are!

I was the out-of-town driver and, since we were battling a massive flow of traffic (approximately 326 lanes inbound), my passenger's job was to help watch for signs.

"We need 290," I said, easing into the flow of traffic. "There's a split up ahead, so help me watch. OK? 290."

"OK," my co-pilot chirped. "We're headed to 90."

"Right, 290."

"There's a sign!" she shouted. "We're in the wrong lane, we need to get over — way over — to the far right!

"What sign?" I snapped. "I didn't see a sign."

"Well, it was right back there, and we only have a half mile. Hurry; I think you can make it."

"Are you sure it said 290?"

"Yes, it said to 90!"

We were clinging to the edge of the far left lane. Each and every lane of traffic to the right of us was hurtling along at Mach 2, directly into the blinding glare of the morning sun. They graciously left a quarter-inch stopping distance between vehicles.

"Hold on," I yelled. My co-pilot gripped the arm rests and I gripped the steering wheel. We swerved and skidded across three-hundred twenty-five lanes of traffic and bullied our way into the far right lane. All in a distance of only eighteen inches.

"I didn't see the 290 sign," I wheezed. "I'm glad you spotted it."

I caught my breath and noticed a light sweat breaking across my forehead.

"Hey! Wait a minute!" I yelled. "This says we're going

to 90. We don't want to go to 90. We want 290!"

"I GOT US TO 90!" she yelled, clutching the dashboard.

"NO! NOT to 90 — 290! Give me the map!"

"YOU CAN'T READ THE MAP WHEN YOU'RE DRIVING!" she screamed.

"No, but I can HIT you with it!"

"Listen to me — 290. Do you understand? 290!"

"Yes, I understand. Do you understand? I got us to 90!"

"No, we don't want to go to 90, we want to go TOOOOO 290."

"Ooooooh," she said. "In that case — and you're not going to like this — we need to get back to the far left."

The traffic, which was only mildly surly before, had now turned ugly. Trucks were pushing little compact cars like crumbs into a dust pan. SUVs had metal spikes poking from their wheels and a VW bug up ahead sprayed an oil slick and roofing nails from its rear exhaust. What's more, a sedan sped by with an artillery gun mounted to the sunroof.

"I'm going for it. HANG ON!"

We careened wildly, lurching ahead of trucks and sliding between minivans. We did a 360 and miraculously ended up pointed in the right direction in the far left lane — the 290 lane.

Together time. Utterly exhausting.

The (Woof) Consolation Prize

For some reason, when your kids leave home and get places of their own, they think you want to babysit their animals. I guess they see a pet as a consolation prize. You can't have us anymore, but here, we'll loan you our four-footed friend that piddles in the entryway when he gets excited. If I had my choice of consolation prizes, I'd take new luggage, or cookware over a dog that drags his bottom across my carpet.

We have been babysitting our son's mutt while our son and his wife are on a short trip. The dog is not only smart, he is manipulative.

The dog came from a rescue shelter with a bad hip, no hair on his tail and low thyroid. He turned on the charm, wagged his hairless rat tail, and made himself irresistible. We can only hope that our son will be as good to us one day as he is to the dog. Like the dog, we too show signs of beginning to fall apart. (We are still working on turning on the charm.)

The first thing the dog did when released into my care was bound into the house and jump on the sofa. He shot me a defiant look that said, "I'm away from home. I'm lonely and insecure. You're not so cold as to make me get off the sofa, are you?"

"Off the sofa!" I barked.

I wasn't going to stand guard in the family room, so I opened magazines and spread them all over the sofa as a deterrent to the dog.

When I came home that afternoon, there was the dog paging through a Talbot's catalog. He had also pulled a membership card out of America's First Freedom.

I was dog-tired and wanted to sit down on my own sofa. But every time I picked up a magazine to clear a space for myself, the dog jumped to his feet and poised to lunge. As soon as I put the magazine back on the sofa, the dog sat back down. Up, down, up, down.

I left the magazines on the sofa and casually walked across the room and sat in a chair that has never interested the dog. Quick as a wink the dog was on my lap. Smiling. Panting. Gloating. Breathing his bad doggie breath directly into my face. He had me now because, technically, he wasn't on the furniture; he was on me, the owner of the furniture. Score one for the canine.

That night the manipulator padded into our bedroom about 1 a.m. "What's the matter?" I asked. "The rug by the front door isn't good enough for you?" I turned on the light. It looked like a tear glistening in his left eye.

I suddenly thought of my brother-in-law who is not a dog lover. He used to smile at their family dog and in a cheerful voice say, "You're going to die before I do." The dog did die. My sister-in-law had the dog cremated and put his ashes in an urn, which now sits next to a framed portrait of the dog on top of their entertainment center. I have often wondered if my brother-in-law will fare as well.

I dragged myself out of bed, got the dog a towel, and put it by the closet door. "Make yourself at home," I said.

I turned off the light and heard a scratch, scratch, scratch. I turned on the light. The dog had moved the towel next to my side of the bed. He looked at me pleadingly, longingly, lovingly.

"No," I said. "Go to sleep." I could feel his brown eyes staring at me in the dark. I was determined the dog with the bad hip and low thyroid would not make me feel guilty in my own home. At peace with my conscience, I fell right to sleep. In only three hours.

The first thing the next morning, I removed two magazines from the sofa and surrendered one cushion.

Dip Cone

As empty nesters, the husband and I are spending a little more time together now. We get along very well, especially when you consider that we are fundamentally incompatible. But every once in awhile, we just seem to needle each other. Here's an example:

We are on our way to a special event an hour out of town. The husband is wearing suit pants, a crisp white shirt and a tie, and has his suit coat in the back seat with plans to put it on once we arrive.

If there are stages of life, I am officially in the "Thirsty Stage." I don't know why. I just am.

I ask the husband if we have time to whip through a fast food joint so I can get something to drink. He says sure, and maybe he'll get an ice cream cone.

"But you're wearing a white shirt," I say. I may have

said it in a slightly naggy tone of voice.

He looks at me, steels his eyes, smiles, and says, "A chocolate dip cone."

"You can't eat a chocolate dip cone when you're driving and wearing a white shirt!" That one I said in a real naggy tone of voice.

I have inadvertently issued a challenge. This is a mistake because the man has latent juggling abilities.

Every morning, the husband takes two cups of coffee from the house to drink in the car. He takes my breakable pottery mugs. My brother-in-law (the same one that dissed the family dog), is an executive for Thermos. We have an entire cabinet full of Thermos travel mugs, but the husband says, "Coffee does not taste the same out of stainless steel." So he takes two of my pottery mugs, one to teeter on the dashboard at an angle, and the other to wedge into the cup holder. He takes the speed bump out of the subdivision at thirty and never spills.

"Your number is up," I snap. "Maybe when your shirt has chocolate on it you can just carry my pink purse in front of your chest. Or wear your suit coat backward."

He just smiles and orders a Diet Coke for me and a chocolate dip cone for himself. He unfolds three napkins, and tucks them into the collar of his shirt one at a time.

On the first bite he makes a clean break. We hang a hard right out of the lot, accelerate on the entrance ramp, and hit seventy on the interstate. Driver, cone, and white shirt are still intact.

He takes another bite. The chocolate cracks right down the center. The back wedge wobbles toward his chest. He bobs low and makes a mid-air catch worthy of an instant replay.

One mile later, he is down to three jagged chunks of chocolate teetering above the cone. Bing, bing, bing, he knocks them off and wolfs them down rapid fire.

I'm waiting . . . just waiting . . . but nothing — he's got the dip cone under control. Then, he turns to gloat and a big drip of ice cream smacks the napkin covering his shirt.

"What it gonna be, Big Guy? My necklace or my purse?"

He lifts the napkins. The ice cream has gone through napkin one, napkin two, napkin three, and soaked a small spot on his tie — in the center of a dark brown paisley. It is undetectable! He thrusts his arms into a victory stance and makes a rushing air sound like thousands of dip cone fans are cheering wildly.

We arrive at our destination and exit the car.

Who has two big spots of Diet Coke on the bottom of her jacket?

Laptop Breakfast

One of the many surprises of having the kids grown and gone is that we find ourselves breaking a lot of the house rules.

We don't always put our dirty dishes directly into the dishwasher. Sometimes we let them pile up in the sink and get hard and crusty overnight.

I occasionally hang in the refrigerator, letting the cold air escape while watching that little white bulb burn for no apparent reason. There's something about doing that that makes me feel rich.

Last night — hang on to your chair — we both left our shoes *on the stairs* WHERE ANYONE COULD TRIP OVER THEM!

I know, I know. Call us wild and crazy. He's Wild and

I'm Crazy.

For some reason, we don't feel compelled to abide by the rules we imposed on the kids. This probably says something about democracy, fascism, and benevolent dictatorships, but I'm not sure what.

I used to picture that, when we had the house to ourselves, the husband and I would linger over morning coffee together at the breakfast table. Never mind the fact that I'm not a coffee drinker, I envisioned us sipping java, tossing sections of the newspaper back and forth, pointing out items of note, laughing about cartoons, and marveling at how quickly I can solve the Jumble.

That scene rarely happens. Instead, in complete violation and total disregard of the Unplugged-While-You-Eat rule, we are more likely to have breakfast with our laptops.

There we sit. His and hers. Coffee, tea, and PCs.

The only things we toss across the table are power cords.

"Look at this picture from the game," the husband says, already browsing while my machine is still waking up.

"What? You want me to run around the table to look at a picture?" I ask.

We both laugh.

At least we still know not to get up from our chairs before a meal is finished.

"Send me the link," I say, clicking away, having finished the local paper online and now navigating through the Wall Street Journal.

"Whoa," I say. "You'd like this one. Hold on, I just emailed you an article."

"Hmmmm," the husband says with great concern.

"Lose your connection?" I ask.

"No, it looks like rain moving in," he says. "Go to Weatherundergound and zoom in on the regional radar."

Of course, that's much simpler than looking out the window, where we would see ominous dark clouds gathering in the northwest, notice the wind whipping through the trees, and a stray cat clawing at the back door seeking shelter.

"Hey, did you remember I'll be out of town a few days?" I ask. "Go to the family Google calendar. I posted it online. Oh, and did you see the kids put new pictures on Facebook?"

"Already seen them," he says. "You talked to any of them lately?"

"I received a lovely e-card from the youngest just yesterday and the oldest now follows me on Twitter."

I feel the husband's eyes boring into me, but I am now engrossed in an opinion piece

"I'm sorry. Did you say something?" I ask. "I was reading Charles Krauthammer."

"I said I think we may have a problem," he says. "You know what they say."

"The family that texts together, stays together?" I ask.

"No, we ought to stop meeting like this."

The Ins and Outs of Leaving Home

It probably won't be in the Guinness Book of World Records, but the husband and I set a record last week. We pulled out of the driveway on our first trip out of the house.

We often back out of the garage and park in the drive-way for a minute or two, maybe three or four, or sometimes even half a day, because one of us has forgotten something inside the house and needs to make a trip back in.

Coupons. The coffeemaker still turned on. The list.

On particularly bad days we have been known to make as many as four trips back inside. Each. We save those special occasions for pre-dawn trips out of town, when the husband can also alert the neighbors to our ineptness by accidently setting off the car's panic alarm on the key fob.

One day we were both opening and shutting car doors, making numerous trips back inside for additional items that kept springing to mind, and we passed each other in the front hall. We agreed if we each made another trip inside, we would meet in the kitchen, because it would then be time for lunch.

We appear organized and we think we are organized, but we can never seem to leave home without at least one mad dash back inside.

Do you have the library books? No, I thought you had the library books.

Was the toilet still running? What? The toilet was running?

And so it goes — check the back door, retrieve a bottled water, sunglasses, a jacket, bills to drop off at the corner mailbox.

On occasion we rattle off a list of things each other might have forgotten. That may sound considerate, but often the tone is not so much helpful as it is intensely competitive.

Him: "Reading glasses?"

Me: "Always. Cell phone?"

Him: "Absolutely. Umbrella?"

Me: "Of course. Bank deposit slip?"

I can tell from his face that he has forgotten it and yell, "Gotcha," instantly scoring twenty-five points and securing me a spot in the bonus round.

If there is an item we have both forgotten and it is of mutual benefit, the question is who has to go back inside. The rules of return are that if the driver has car keys in the ignition and the car is running, the return trip defaults to the passenger. If, however, the passenger is cradling a hot coffee, the rules for return are open for discussion.

Sure, we have had efficient days when it looks like we're making a clean break the first time out of the house, but then we reach the stop sign at the end of the block and nearly always discover we have forgotten something. People thought it was spectacular when Jack Bauer did a getaway chase completely in reverse on "24." Please. He learned it from us.

Sometimes we leave the neighborhood and get all the way to a nearby busy intersection before we realize what we have forgotten, necessitating another return home. On those occasions the husband will drive home and back the car into the driveway, making it look like we are positioned for a speedy getaway.

Believe me, it will never happen.

Hey, Isn't That . . . ?

The husband has a knack for spotting famous people. I have a knack for thinking I spot famous people and being unwilling to admit that I am wrong.

When we took a trip to Montana, the husband spotted Phil Jackson, former coach of the Los Angeles Lakers, walking through the Kalispell airport. He was pretty excited and thought I'd be excited, too; but even when he pointed out the coach, I didn't recognize him.

However, I did recognize Jim Nabors on that same trip. The husband said I didn't see Jim Nabors, I just thought I did because the locals said Jim Nabors had a vacation home in the area. I still say it was Jim Nabors walking his dog down the street.

My problem is that when I really do see famous people, I often don't know who they are. Once I was on flight with a team from the WNBA. I asked my seatmates, who had their names on their jackets, what team they were with and I thought they said the Detroit Shot. I opened my book and kept my head down.

I relayed the players' names to the husband, who immediately recognized them and informed me they are the Detroit Shock, not the Detroit Shot.

That confusion aside, I am pretty sure that I saw Queen Latifah at our Wal-Mart recently, but the husband says celebrities don't shop at Wal-Mart. I say it's entirely possible they do because even celebrities need toilet paper and paper towels.

And then I saw Hillary Clinton at Macy's.

"You couldn't have seen Hillary at Macy's," the husband said. "She's in the Mideast brokering peace."

"Well, not on Wednesday she wasn't. She was trying on black leather boots."

I also spotted Lady Gaga coming out of the local high school. Her hair was in a big purple Mohawk and she had on a red leather body suit with chains wrapped around her neck and was headed into Steak 'n Shake.

I also know beyond a shadow of a doubt that I saw Dolly Parton at a Cracker Barrel last spring. Such a sweet thing. She was manning the hostess stand and gave us a real nice table near the fireplace.

The husband likes to remind me that he has a much

longer, and far more legitimate, track record of spotting famous people. When he was in college he ran into Mohammed Ali.

That's nice, but I can up the ante. I wouldn't want this to go too far because it could cause real chaos at Jiffy Lube, but Trace Adkins helped change the oil on my car. He even put the little plastic sticker on the windshield to remind me when to come in again.

Last week I was as shocked as anybody to see Brad Pitt at our grocery store.

When I informed the husband, he said, "Sure you saw Brad Pitt at the grocery. On a tabloid cover, right?"

"No, he wasn't on a tabloid cover, Mister-I'm-the-Only-One-Who-Sees-Famous-People. He was carrying groceries out to the car for Betty White."

The Pond and the Bear

When your kids leave home, your entire pattern of living changes.

There are fewer voices and faces to greet good morning and bid good night.

When you are in bed and the clock approaches midnight, you start to do the where-are-they, when-will-they-be-back, and how-many-are-home-now count. Then you realize everybody who will be home is home.

Two.

You have a four-bedroom house with only one bedroom in use.

The house that was often cramped now seems ridiculously big.

You no longer buy three gallons of milk each week.

You buy one gallon and keep checking the expiration date.

Lettuce spoils, bananas turn brown, and a small rump roast lasts an entire week.

Grocery shopping changes. Cooking changes. Laundry changes.

There are new luxuries. You can pull your car into the garage without first moving two others in the driveway. You can use the blow dryer without having to listen for another blow dryer running in another bathroom, because together they will trip the circuit breaker every time.

You and your spouse get to know each other again. Yet, your conversation topics seem to have dwindled.

Who are you again? Exactly what is it we have in common?

There was a moment we were coming home one night and the husband was unlocking the door and I was standing close and we kissed. It was like being 17 and on a first date. But it wasn't a first date, it was just a couple who hadn't had an extended pause together in a very long time.

Being a twosome again takes you back to when you first met and past all the things that have transpired between then and now. You realize you never looked this far into the future. You never really imagined what it would be like when it was just the two of you again. Oh sure, you thought about it on large scale in a hypothetical way, but it was never this real, this specific, or this quiet.

Who was he anyway?

An even better question, who was I?

"We've turned into the Bickersons," a friend lamented after her last one left home. Three years later, they divorced.

Much of a mother's work vanishes with the kids. A big part of her is packed in so many cardboard boxes and tossed in the back of a car.

It was a pleasure to be needed. It was a joy to help. It was fun to watch them mature and wonderful to listen.

And now it's just you and Mr. Conversationalist over there who hasn't spoken a word in fifty minutes.

Did we know we'd be so all-consumed by jobs, work, and everyday demands that the tender bonds that first united us would grow a brittle crust?

We were hiking around Jordan Pond in Acadia National Park in Maine on our first getaway with just the two of us, as I was thinking such thoughts. We were there before the tourist season and had the entire trail and pond to ourselves. The husband was alternately lagging behind and dashing ahead, framing photos, making pictures. It was spring and small green sprouts were pushing up through the debris that littered winter's floor. Buds on understory trees had opened wide. Hibernation season was over. With a stretch and a yawn, the entire earth was awakening.

The trail that circles Jordan Pond alternately breaks into the sunshine and weaves through the dark covering of the forest. It's a long hike. A long, quiet, desolate hike.

Following the trail into the trees, a rutting sound bounced off the densely wooded hillside. I grabbed a big stick. It was a pitiful excuse for a weapon, but I might be able to poke an eye with it, or at the very least tickle the wild beast's funny bone. The husband caught up with me and heard the sound, too. Something large was lurking in the woods.

"Do you plan to fight a bear with that stick?" he smirked.

"If I have to," I said indignantly. "What do you propose? If something comes charging out of the woods, what is your plan?"

"You take off running," he said.

"Why would I take off running?" I ask.

"You'd run for help."

"And what would you do?"

"I'd stay with the bear so you could get away."

Just like that, an accumulation of lingering resentments and petty grudges brought about by the endless busyness of family life and unanswered questions about the unknown and the future melted away. Life would be different now, but we still had what we started with. I was still loved by the one I chose to love all those years ago.

3

EVEN THE CAKE WAS IN TIERS

Here Comes the Groom

When I had given birth to our first child, a son, the nurse-midwife asked my husband if he would like to cut the cord. There is a reason they ask fathers to cut the umbilical cord. They are able to do it quickly.

< Snip >

For mothers, cutting the cord often takes a little longer. Somewhere in the neighborhood of twenty years.

By nature, mothers are reluctant to share their sons. We raise them with hopes they will be strong and independent and have families of their own one day, but we also raise them with secret desires that they will always be ours.

When you attend the parent-teacher conference and the first-grade teacher shows you the class book — the book in which your son has drawn a picture of a shark jumping out of the water with the pretty young teacher's feet sticking out of the sharks' mouth, you pretend to be mildly appalled, but a part of you is glad. You are glad it is the teacher pictured having the Jaws experience and not you, hence proving you still hold first place in his heart.

The cord again stretches taut in sixth grade, when at Christmas time he announces he has bought a giant red-and-white candy cane for a girl and will give it to her on the bus.

"What did she say?" you ask later.

"Nothing." He lowers his eyes and walks away.

You resist the urge to find the girl and pinch her little twelve-year-old nose right off her face.

At least he knows the female he can truly trust, the one who will always be there for him.

The cord stretches again when the boy goes on an all-day field trip and forgets his lunch. He calls to ask if you will bring it to school. "I'll be outside, just slow down, and toss it out the car window."

You find comfort knowing he still needs you for the little things like food, shelter, and clean underwear.

Then one day you realize that the things he needed you to do for him, he is now doing for himself: cooking, cleaning, paying bills.

Living on one's own may well be the most educational

part of college.

He is home over break. The family is in the kitchen and I am dumping the trash, when his grandmother asks what his intentions are with the girl he has recently begun dating.

"Glad you asked, Grandma." Out of the corner of my eye, I see him pull a ring box from the pocket of his jeans. My life flashes before me, looking remarkably similar to junk mail and cantaloupe rinds when I realize this is not my life, but that I am simply falling headfirst into the trash can.

The husband runs to the stairs and yells to the girls, "Your brother is getting married!" They rush into the kitchen and yell, "Congratulations! To whom?"

He says she is the girl he has been dating for twenty-eight days. He says this proudly as though four solid weeks, just two days short of a full month, should put our minds at ease.

"Well, I think that's just great," my mother says. "If you know she's the one, she's the one. Your grandfather and I didn't have a long engagement."

"Don't listen to her," I say. "Theirs is a relationship built on lies."

They met New Year's Eve at a dance hall. Dad asked Mom if she ever came to the midweek dance. She said no, because she taught school. Dad said he didn't either, because he worked at a gas station on Wednesday nights.

On Wednesday night they were both back at the dance hall.

"That was just the first lie I caught her in," Dad said laughing.

"We met in January, were engaged in March, and married in August," Mom said.

Actually, our son had known this girl more than 28 days. They had dated briefly his sophomore year in college and decided they were just friends. Her family lived on wooded property in the southern part of the state. Despite the breakup, our son remained on good terms with her father and periodically went down to their property to hike and camp, and visit with her dad.

We referred to her as the lovely one that got away, although her father seemed to be working out nicely.

Grandma and Grandpa went home the next day and we were still somewhat stunned, if not reeling from shock.

"You just will have graduated college. What will you do for a job?" we asked.

"I had eight offers for internships; I'll find a job."

"What will you do for money?"

"We've been poor college students, we can be poor newlyweds."

For every question he had an answer.

"I've got a crockpot," he volunteered.

As though owning a crockpot was a mark of financial security.

"Yes, but will you have anything to put in it?" I asked.

"She's totally committed," he said with great passion.

"COMMITTED TO WHAT?" we yelled in unison.

"TO ME!" he yelled, thrusting his arms into the air.

The fact is, there is a sense of loss when a son leaves home to make a home of his own. It is the end of a chapter, the closing of an era.

Acknowledging that the past is the past is how you clear space and make room for the new. There will be a new family member, a new dimension, new laughter, new warmth and new life.

He is once again home for the weekend, standing by the front door, waiting for her to arrive. I steal a glance and see him as a little boy with tousled hair, muddy tennis shoes, a skateboard, and G.I. Joes. How can this kid be a young man about to marry?

"She's here!" he says, to no one in particular. "The love of my life," and flies out the door.

< Snip >

Register This

B etween four of us who are close in our neighborhood, we have had seven weddings among our ten children in a span of several years. When your children, your friend's children, and your children's friends approach their mid- and late-twenties, you become a frequent visitor at the wedding registry kiosks at the big box houseware stores.

Registering for a wedding today is an entirely different experience from when I was a young bride-to-be. When you registered eons ago, your mother went with you to the fine china section of a big department store. You sat down in straight-back chairs in front of a grand desk on thick carpet. Behind the desk was a prim and proper graduate of the Emily Post School of Etiquette who was wearing a Channel suit, the faint scent of Estee Lauder, and had eyeglasses hanging from a pearl chain dangling around her neck.

The registry attendant opened an enormous book, donned her half-moon glasses, and asked the name of the china pattern you had selected, the name of the everyday pottery you had selected, if you had selected flatware and, most importantly, your colors.

A girl had colors in those days. You didn't get married without colors. As soon as you were engaged, people asked, "What are your colors?" They didn't mean the colors of the bridesmaids' dresses; they meant the colors you planned to use for home décor. What were the colors for your bath and your kitchen?

Colors were a big decision. My colors were earth tones, at least that is what the attendant entered into the extremely large book. I said brown, but she wrote earth tones. Maybe when your glasses dangle from a pearl chain, you're too refined to write brown in a registry, so you rename it earth tones, which is a nicer way of saying I planned to decorate using the color of dirt.

In any case, brown, or earth tones, was a bold decision on my part. My mother's generation had decorated their kitchens in turquoise in the Fifties and then in the Sixties and Seventies moved to avocado green, harvest gold, and autumn orange. And now I was making a wild and radical break, navigating uncharted color swatches by going with brown. Earth tones. Dirt.

At each of my showers, I received all things brown: brown hand towels, brown bath towels, brown shower curtain, brown placemats, brown throw rugs, brown napkin rings. When you registered in those days, there was still an element of surprise to the gifts. You didn't know what was in the gift box, but in my case I knew it would be brown.

Nobody could envision the day when brides-to-be would register by scanning an entire home living store with a small laser gun capable of tagging everything in stock in under forty minutes.

Pity the young man dragged along for the full bridal registry experience. You've seen these couples in the store. They start out all dewy and fresh, but with each subsequent crossing of your paths, the groom-to-be looks a little more weary, a little more disheveled, a little more pained.

"Look, an OXO peeler! Don't you love it?" the female squeals.

The guy says nothing. No response. Nada.

Beep, she scans it.

"A garlic press!" she giggles.

Silence. He wonders if the game is in the second half now.

Beep, she scans the garlic press.

"French rolling pin or standard rolling pen, hon?"

An entire afternoon of his life that he will never get back.

She scans both rolling pins. Beep. Beep.

"Flip top trash can or Simplehuman Profile 10-Liter Step Can?"

Please, please let this end.

By the time the bride-to-be has dragged her fiancé to the section with mirrors, picture frames, and lamps, the looks on both their faces say Jimmy the Greek is laying odds they'll never make it to the altar.

The bridal registries of today make shopping for wedding gifts practical and convenient, but they also take some of the fun and creativity out of shopping. You don't really have to think about the couple, ponder their personalities or interests, consider what might delight or amuse them, because they've already told you: king-size sheet set, 800-thread count, Egyptian cotton; Vera Wang Love Knots Double 5 x 7 frame from Wedgewood; Delonghi Electric Citrus Juicer; Cuisinart Stainless Steel Ice Cream Maker; Homedics Digital Scale; Precise Clean Electric Toothbrush, and a Black and Decker crosscut paper shredder.

Let's not overlook the wedding registries that indicate the bride and groom will accept gift cards. It's like registering for money. Why, yes, we would enjoy fifties, hundreds, and twenties; no fives or tens, please.

At times it seems a little impersonal. A little grabby even. Maybe I've just printed out a few too many registries with a $500 vacuum on the first page.

Eighty-dollar water goblets also have been known to drive me over the edge. *Oh, please. You really need ten eighty-dollar water goblets? That's almost a thousand dollars, and judging from Facebook, you seem to be very at ease with those big red plastic tumblers.*

Despite the attitude a twenty-page bridal registry sometimes triggers, I sincerely enjoy bridal showers. A bridal shower is fun because a bridal shower is insane. It is the only time in a woman's life when she will squeal with delight at something as mundane as a plastic lettuce knife or a dish towel.

I've often said you can tell what stage of life a woman is at by looking at her kitchen towels.

Shortly after our oldest daughter was married, I pulled a load of clothes from her dryer for her and found the cutest all-cotton dish towels embroidered with the days of the week. Each and every one of them was wrinkled in a tight ball.

"What do you do with these?" I asked.

"I iron them," she deadpanned.

She did. She misted them, ironed them, creased them, put them in order, and placed them in a kitchen drawer. But then again, her measuring spoons still nestled, her measuring cups still stacked, and not a single plastic spatula had a melted edge resembling the coastline of Florida. What a newlywed.

The woman whose kitchen drawer is crammed full of flour sack and nubby terry cloth towels folded at odd angles is a woman who has been at the game for awhile. If the towels are stained with coffee, spaghetti sauce, and mustard, you are looking at the disheveled drawer of a busy woman who provides good nutrition for her family.

When you find a woman with children whose kitchen towel drawer is neat and tidy, filled with spotless, perfectly folded organic cotton towels in a rainbow of the latest citrus colors, you can be certain of one thing: The family eats out a lot.

The towel drawer with dish towels featuring pictures of barnyard animals, woodland creatures, autumn leaves, cheery snowmen, Valentine hearts, and an oven mitt that looks like a wide mouth bass is a drawer belonging to a teacher or a grandma.

We women have a mysterious relationship with the towels of our lives. Our towels change as we change. Our towels age as we age.

My mother had two kitchen towels hanging from a shelf in her kitchen. They were starched white cotton with crisp black needlework. The one on the left said, "Martha Stewart Doesn't Live Here." The one on the right said, "Inside Every Old Person is a Young Person Wondering What Happened."

The woman whose kitchen towel drawer has a mix

of cotton blue towels faded to gray, red towels faded to pink, and half of the towels are so threadbare it's a toss-up whether they belong in the kitchen drawer or the rag bag, is a woman who has likely crossed into her fifties.

She's due for an update.

Somebody, please, give the woman a kitchen shower. Better yet, have her fill out a registry and turn her loose at a home goods store with one of those little laser scanners.

But Will They Have Stories?

When we had our taxes figured, our accountant mentioned his daughter was getting married. He said the rental cost for chairs alone was approaching several thousand dollars.

He explained the guests would need chairs by the Canal Plaza, where the ceremony would be, in addition to chairs inside the state Historical Society building, where the reception would be.

Our accountant's idea, and granted he's a CPA, not a wedding planner (but it made perfect sense to us), was to assign each guest a chair and tell them to keep it with them at all times.

"Of course, a BYOC event," I mused. "Bring your own chair."

"Exactly," he said.

His daughter didn't go for it. Neither did his wife.

Call it coincidence, but our fee for this year's tax service jumped considerably.

After hearing our accountant's ideas about guests lugging their chairs with them, we will never again take for granted having a place to sit at a wedding or a reception.

We were seated (in lovely chairs I might add) at a beautiful wedding reception when someone at the table asked where the bride and groom were going on their honeymoon.

A voice in the know said they were going on some cruise to some island somewhere. It was one of those places that is hot and humid and has an exotic name that sounds like a mixed drink or liqueur — something like Tahiti or Daiquiri or Kahlua.

"That's nice," said the woman to my right, taking a sip from her water goblet.

"That's nice," said the woman to my left, spearing a cherry tomato with her salad fork.

They both said it with all the excitement of a woman scheduling a mammogram.

There was a time when people jumped up and down over news of an ocean cruise. Being on a big ship, drinking out of a coconut, and ice sculptures gracing the buffet used to be a big deal. Now it seems part and parcel of the entire wedding package.

Honeymoon in Hawaii?

Yawn.

Going to the Caribbean?

Yes, could you pass the Sweet'N Low, please?

"So, where did you go on your honeymoon?" I asked the couple to my left.

She giggled and he answered.

"That was twenty-eight years ago. We had just graduated from college. I was going on to grad school and we didn't have much money. We were married in Chicago and stayed at a hotel by the O'Hare Airport."

"I got sick," the wife said. "He spent the weekend sitting on the end of the bed watching baseball games on television."

"Cleveland played the White Sox," he said. "The center fielder for Cleveland had a really good bunt."

"Where did you go on your honeymoon?" I asked the couple to the right.

"I had just finished college and he was in the middle of seminary. He had an internship with a church in Washington, D.C. My grandma lived there, so she cleared out and gave us the keys to her house for a few days. She was a prankster and put wire coat hangers under the sheets."

He laughed.

She laughed.

The entire table laughed, and the woman turned as red as the cherry tomato still on her fork.

I asked another couple where they went for their honeymoon. "We went camping," he said.

"It rained every day and I'm still mad," she said. They both laughed.

"Where did you go on your honeymoon?" someone asked me.

"We came back to the Midwest to get married," I answered. "The flight taking us back to our jobs on the West Coast made a stop in San Francisco so we did, too. We stayed at the Mark Twain hotel. I found it in a travel book. It wasn't too expensive and we thought it would be a good place for journalists.

"Turned out it was directly across the street from the bus station. It was a flophouse. There were cigarette burns in the sheets and holes in the ceiling, so you could see through the roof. To top all it off, the airline lost our luggage. We changed hotels the next day."

Everyone was laughing and shaking their heads.

"I suppose this young couple will fly first class," someone said.

"Probably."

"I suppose they'll have lovely accommodations and a beautiful room."

"Probably."

"I suppose there will be gourmet food and polite porters."

"Probably."

Poor kids.

Hope they have some decent stories to tell thirty years from now.

Dressing Up and Busting Out

There are blatant inequities when it comes to wedding attire for males and females. Men do not try on tux after tux, tossing them over the fitting room door with sighs of exasperation, rejecting cummerbunds five, ten, and twenty at a time, vowing to give up carbs, and try Pilates.

Men walk into a formal wear store, have a few strategic measurements taken, and return the day before the wedding to pick up their penguin suits. The entire process takes roughly eight minutes.

By contrast, Columbus sailed to the New World in half the time it takes a woman to find a dress for a special occasion.

As a woman who was soon to be an MOB (mother of the bride), I have to say it was great fun watching the bride-to-be try on dresses. It was great fun watching the brides-maids try on dresses. It was great fun chumming with the flower girl, who said her mother told her that her job was to, "drop flower petals, walk proud, and not goof around."

But when it was time for the mother of the bride to begin the dress hunt, the fun quotient plummeted like a diver springing off the high board.

On the upside, preliminary dress shopping could be done on the internet. You could peruse dresses and deter-mine which ones might be worth trying on in the store. Yet, there seemed to be considerable disparity between how a dress looked on the computer screen and how it looked in the fitting room.

The silver dress with the straight skirt and square-cut jacket, the one that whispered understated elegance online, took on a different look when covering my actual person. It had the distinct look of a stainless steel refrigerator. The dazzling jewel trim on the right pocket could even pass for the ice dispenser.

The flowing gown with the full skirt that looked so graceful online looked like a frock worn by Mary Queen of Scots. "Bring me my scepter! Where is my tea?"

My shopping companion said that my narration was not helpful. I said the models online were probably all seven feet tall and gave up eating solid food when they hit puberty.

The ruffled number with the flounces that looked so sleek and sophisticated on the website looked like a dust ruffle without end in front of the three-way mirror.

The dark green suit that was breathtaking on my monitor looked like a pup tent. The teal blue number guaranteed to camouflage middle-age "flaws" could have doubled as a slipcover for Yankee Stadium.

It was a nix on the black number with the long train and long sleeves — a little too Addams Familyish, and a no go on the one with the ostrich feathers — there would be no fan dancing. The halter that plunged to the belly button was a reject while still on the hanger, and the jungle print with the slit to the upper thigh was returned to the rack as well.

I was ready to call it a day when the daughter shopping with me whipped into the dressing room with one more outfit. "I think this is it," she said.

"That's what you said 300 dresses ago."

She zipped it up and pronounced it "the one."

At that point I could have been wearing mechanic's coveralls with Bubba written across the chest and she would have said it was "the one."

"It might make me look like a cake topper," I said. "What do you think?"

"You'll make a good cake topper. I say you should buy it."

My shopping companion, our youngest daughter, knows something of the hazards of special event dresses. She has been a bridesmaid in nine weddings. That's right, nine puffy, fluffy, slinky, strapless, backless, tea-length, floor-length dresses she will likely never wear again. And yet each time she is asked to be in another friend's wedding, she is delighted to say yes.

She is going over her budget, calculating how much money she has with which to purchase a car, and I take the opportunity to point out how much all these weddings are costing her. "Do you realize," I say calmly, "the amount you spend per wedding? Say the dress is $200, shoes $50. You're expected to host a shower, there goes another $100 easy. You overspend on shower and wedding gifts, so add another $100 and at least $50 more if you have to have your hair done. That's a conservative average of $500. You've spent $4,500 on weddings."

She's nodding along, so I seize the moment and say, "I really think you could start saying no when someone invites you to be in their wedding. Offer to work the guest book.

"Let's practice," I say. "I'll pretend to be one of your many friends who wants you to be in her wedding." I hold out my thumb and pinkie like I'm talking on the phone and gush, "Oooooooh I'm getting married in June and I'd love for you to be a bridesmaid!"

To which she says, "I'd love to! What color are the dresses?"

Oh, fine.

Of all the bridesmaid dresses she has worn, the most memorable was the one that held her hostage. It was a knee-length maroon number. She'd picked the dress up from an alteration shop where it had undergone a nip and tuck, returned to her apartment, and tried on the dress. In the world of bridesmaids dresses, it had been a good one, which meant, "reasonably priced." In other words, surprisingly cheap. She zipped up the bridesmaid dress and the zipper caught.

When she tried to free the zipper, the zipper split. The zipper was at a standstill halfway up and halfway down the middle of her back. There was no pulling the fitted dress off overhead and no slithering out of the bottom.

When she called, I thought I could talk her through the dress crisis by phone. I'm usually good at that kind of thing — calm, reassuring. I said, "Ha, ha, ha, ha! You're kidding, right?"

After she tried for a good half an hour to get out of the dress, I finally drove across town and worked on the zipper myself for half an hour. No success. She was trapped. It looked like the old saying might actually be true: always a bridesmaid, never a bride.

I calmly announced we should call the fire department.

I didn't really think we should call the fire department, but using a strategy our son had often used, I started out with the worst-case scenario, thinking she'd take the real news better. The real news was that we would have to go back to the tailor that had done the alteration. He was the only one who could help.

The alteration shop happened to be in an area of the city heavily populated by young people and, with the exception of two inches, the back of the dress was now fully vented.

"I can't go out like this!" she shrieked. "What if I see someone I know?"

I didn't point out the obvious, that if she did see someone she knew, it would give them something highly entertaining to talk about for weeks to come.

She grabbed a rain coat and sunglasses. It was sunny and seventy-eight.

I said it was a great cover and no one would notice.

The lies mothers tell.

We raced to the alternation shop and found a parking place. We then walked three blocks filled with people wearing shorts, T-shirts, and flip flops, and young mothers applying SPF 95 sunscreen to babies. Meanwhile, the recluse next to me had her head down and was clutching the collar of her raincoat high around her neck.

Two tailors and a seamstress, all of whom hail from Germany, emerged from the back room. They saw the figure wrapped in a heavy coat and sunglasses and considered it might be a robbery. We explained the situation and she removed the coat. One by one, they cautiously approached.

"Vat vee have heh is a cheap zippuh," said the first.

"Yah. Cheap zippuh," said the second.

"Yah. Cheap zippuh," said the third.

They took turns pulling on the cheap zipper. The first gave it a try, the second gave it a try. Then the third positioned himself to pull on the zipper while the other two positioned themselves to pull on him. "On da count dah tree!" the tailor yelled. Nothing.

"At least it's a color you look good in," I offered.

One of the gentlemen tailors slipped behind the curtain and returned with pliers. With several clicks, some muttering and a twist, he snipped the zipper without ruining the dress.

The tailor put in a good quality zipper and the dress is fine, although the bridesmaid may never recover.

In the end, no matter what your role in a wedding, be it mother of the groom, mother of the bride or a bridesmaid, it's like the flower girl said. "All that really matters is that "you walk proud, and not goof around."

When the Baby Ties the Knot

The baby is getting married. The one that was in nine weddings has been getting ready for her own wedding. The husband has been copying photographs to put together a video for the reception. He made a wonderful pairing of two photographs. In the picture on the left, she is ten-years-old, wearing my mother's old wedding gown, playing dress up, and I am adjusting her veil. In the picture on the right, she is standing in her real wedding gown and I am kneeling on the floor, pinning fasteners for the bustle.

A quarter-inch of space is all that separates sixteen years. The time went exactly that fast.

She is about to take the plunge. Every marriage has an element of jumping off a cliff. You know the other person as well as you can, that he loathes tomatoes and you like them. You do the premarital counseling, read the communication books, then close your eyes and leap. The act of marriage takes grit and courage. Marrying someone is not the same as living with someone. Living together is test driving the car. Marriage is having the guts to buy the car, knowing it is still yours even after the five-year/50,000 mile warranty has expired.

Marriage is a public commitment, a legal contract, and covenant of faith, in which a bride and groom vow before God and witnesses to uphold a lifelong exclusive faithfulness.

It is nerve wracking knowing that the model of marriage your offspring knows best is your very own.

Did she see that marriage is the most important relationship she will ever nurture?

Did she see that the cornerstone of marriage is courtesy? Tone of voice, dear. Ask, don't tell. Suggest, don't demand. The world outside is rough, so be tender.

I hope she heard me say at least once that women do not have to be first responders. Often it's better not to say the first thing that comes into your mind. Or even the second.

I hope she knows I married her father because he's a good man. She's marrying a good man, too. Respect him by speaking well of him, both to him and to others.

I hope she saw the power of the mundane — that

the shared laughs, small surprises, kitchen disasters, and everyday routine are what cement you as a couple. Crises and catastrophes can drive you apart or become part of the mortar that builds your history.

Our daughter and her fiancé will be glowing on their wedding day. I pray they enjoy every moment of the day. I also pray that they will weather the many seasons of marriage and that, one day in the distant future, they find themselves with a few extra pounds, salt and pepper hair, a thousand inside jokes, and still enjoying one another.

Robert Browning said it well: "Grow old along with me. The best is yet to be — the last of life for which the first was meant."

Back, Mom, Back!

You think you let go of your kids when they marry. At least you hope you let go, because it would be rather unsightly to be middle-aged and clinging to the leg of your married child.

When our oldest daughter was married, her entire body was shaking at the altar. It looked certain she was going to faint. I told myself that if she did faint, to stay right where I was. It wouldn't be my place to jump up. Scooping her off the floor would be the role of the groom. And maybe her dad. The groom, or her dad. Maybe the pastor would help. But not Mom.

Back, Mom, back. Good Mom!

I thought I'd let go when the ceremony was over and she nearly floated down the aisle on the arm of her handsome groom in his military dress uniform. They passed beneath the arch of sabers. The last two soldiers crossed sabers and announced the bride and groom could not pass without a kiss. The groom grabbed her, dipped her, and kissed her. The sabers rose, they passed beneath them, and a first lieutenant at the end of the line swatted her on the backside with his saber and shouted, "Welcome to the Army, ma'am."

For eight months I did a fine job of letting go. Eight months after they were married our daughter found out she needed open heart surgery for an aortic aneurysm and a leaking heart valve.

Bam! Back in full mom mode.

I also knew there was a new name being entered on the medical forms she would be filling out for the family member to contact.

I mentioned to a very reserved and refined friend that I wanted to be sensitive to this new balance of power and not overstep my bounds with our new son-in-law, but it was our daughter having open heart surgery.

She looked at me, this mother of three sons, tilted her pretty head, smiled and sweetly said, "I believe I'd say, 'Step aside, son.'"

And then we both laughed.

Our daughter was a physician assistant in cardiology at the time. She knew exactly what was going to happen and what to expect.

Surgery was on her twenty-fifth birthday. Our pastor and a few close friends came to the hospital early that morning so that we could pray together before she went into surgery. We finished praying, filed out of the small room and gathered in the hallway. All of us except for our son-in-law. I looked back. Our daughter was raised up in the hospital bed with IVs and wires attached, heavily sedated, half-conscious, both arms locked around his neck, pleading with him not to go.

I knew then that we had been forever displaced. As it should be, her first and closest alliance was her new husband.

The surgery went well. Happy Birthday.

When the nausea finally subsided and she was able to eat by mouth, both her husband and I were in the room. My instincts were to rush to the food tray, but again the inner voice said, back, Mom, back. Good Mom.

He picked up the fork, loaded a big mound of wobbly green Jell-O, and fed it to her.

Another big blob. I just watched and reminded myself that I was on the B team now. I chuckled inside, because it was actually very, very, sweet.

She whispered something that neither of us could understand.

"What's that?" he said, leaning closer.

"Girl bites," she rasped. "Girl bites."

"I think she means smaller bites," I said. "And the spoon might work better."

He looked at the fork, laughed, and downgraded the size of the bites he was loading on the spoon.

They were cementing together, finding their footing in an unusual and unnerving situation. A young woman was learning how to communicate her needs to her husband and a young man was learning how to care for his wife.

Things went swimmingly on all counts, until they removed the dressing. It was a first look at the raw incision that seemed to run the length of her chest. She was clinical and matter of fact, exchanging medical jargon with the surgeon, but later that evening she had a meltdown about her hair. A complete and total breakdown.

I shampooed and dried her hair and the sobs began to lessen.

I left for the evening and our son-in-law walked me to my car.

"You get it, right?" I asked. "You know that breakdown she's having isn't about her hair. It's about that big incision running down the middle of her chest and wondering if you'll still think she's pretty."

"I thought that might be what was happening," he said. "I get it."

And he did.

It didn't matter if her mother or her father said she was still pretty. It didn't matter if the marquee in Times Square said she was pretty. It only mattered what he thought.

She belonged to him now, the one who fed her girl-size bites of Jell-O, ordered milkshakes for her at midnight, and was going to tell her she was beautiful as soon as he went back to the room.

For better or worse, in sickness and in health.

4

The Life of the Party

The new beginnings, the children taking spouses, and the grandbabies are the good part of getting older. The goodbyes are the sad part. Joy kisses you on one cheek; sorrow on the other.

My mother's death certificate said she was seventy-three years, six months and twenty-nine days old at the time of death. It didn't seem like enough. There were more things we were going to do.

She suffered a brain aneurysm, and when she died it was like she took the party with her. My mother was a personality and a presence. She loved politics and had strong opinions. None of us would have been surprised to turn on a cable news show and see her sitting behind a desk doing commentary. She would have been a hit.

She was also a great storyteller. My mother could describe eating a soda cracker and drinking a glass of tepid water while seated on a metal folding chair and make it sound like you missed the party of the year.

My mother had forty-four nieces and nephews living at the time she died. All of them lived in other states, but nearly all of them came for her funeral. She was respected and loved. She was a woman who knew how to do life.

She was a woman who loved her grandkids more than life itself. When we gave her one of those grandma necklaces years ago, we had no idea a woman could get so much mileage out of a simple gold chain and five little figurines. Mom wore the necklace often and said she loved keeping her grandkids close to her heart. The thing was, you never knew how many grandchildren would be close to her heart.

Some days, all five might be on the chain, other days there might be only be three or four.

"I see one of the grandkids is missing, Mom. What happened?"

"Your brother's youngest smarted off. I took him off the necklace."

She wouldn't really take a grandkid off the necklace, but she would zip their figurine around back, under her collar, where it was all hot and stuffy. She'd tell them when they straightened out, they could rejoin the others.

When I told women friends I encountered that I had recently lost my mom, to a person, those who had lost their mothers, would say, "I lost mine — " and then cite the month, day, and year. It rolled off their tongues.

But, to cheat the sting of death, you must be grateful for the life. So it was, seventy-three years, six months and twenty-nine days.

An older friend said when she lost her mother she cried every day for two years. I thought to myself, that might have been you, but that won't be me. My mother wouldn't want me carrying on like that. I'll recover. I'll be strong again soon.

My friend was right, nearly every day for two years. In the car alone, vacuuming, at the first snow, reaching for the phone, with each changing season, on her birthday and mine.

I once read a quote that stuck in my memory. He who loves much, grieves much. I'm glad I remembered that. It helped a little. But not much.

Appreciate the One You Love

After my mother died, my father said that every man should have a kick in the butt for not appreciating all the things a woman does for him.

A friend who was too young when she lost her husband wondered aloud why more husbands and wives aren't demonstrative with one another.

"Why don't I see husbands putting their arms around their wives? Why aren't you holding hands?" she asked. "Why aren't you cherishing one another?" Tears welled in her eyes.

Why don't we?

No relationship can stay in the honeymoon phase forever, and every relationship has natural ebbs and flows. Yet it has been ages since I put a note in the husband's pocket.

It's been some time since I left for a trip and found he had slipped a new journal and some chocolate in my suitcase.

Recently, I read an author who said we should be so enthralled with loving our spouse that we have little time to ask, "Am I being loved? Am I getting what I need?" It resonated at first, and then it sounded hokey. I wondered if her spouse ever jarred her awake at night snoring because he sounded like a chainsaw?

Our ability to cherish one another gets sandwiched between the demands of work, kids, household chores, bills to pay, calls to make, emails to answer, errands to run. A general state of busyness compresses communication to telegraphic code.

"Hungry?"

"Yeah."

"Mexican?"

"Sure."

The husband recently brought home an armload of treasures from an estate sale. We already have more treasures than we need. His treasures included seven poker dog prints, a worn photograph of the elm tree under which our state constitution was signed, and a very old, large, musty-smelling black and white print with curled edges and a water stain that he thought I might like to hang in the dining room.

Seriously?

It was a line drawing of two Victorian ladies reading a letter and having tea at a small table. It was worn and drab.

And then I remembered my friend who had chastised marrieds for not caring for one another. So I paused and said, "Help me understand why you thought this belonged in the dining room."

"You like tea," he said, "and you often have friends over for tea and you like to entertain. The ladies look like they are enjoying themselves. It reminded me of you and I thought you would like it."

From a different perspective and at a slower pace, maybe it did possess a certain charm.

I said thank you, which is what I should have said at the very first.

Military couples, separated by a deployment, often start their phone calls by saying, "I love you." They say it up front because they never know when the call might be cut off. Maybe the rest of us could take a cue and move the kindness to the front as well. Now, not later.

Dad

After my father had surgery for pancreatic cancer and was told he had six months to live, he came home from the hospital and found some certificates of deposit had come due at the bank. He could renew them for seven months or thirteen — he told me to call the bank and take the thirteen.

Three months after his surgery, we drove him to Nebraska and went out to dinner with one of his brothers, who had been experiencing health problems as well. Afterward, the two brothers stood outside the restaurant in the golden light of the setting sun. They shook hands, each trying to pull the other off balance, slapped one another on the back, laughed heartily, and said, "Let's do this again next year!"

In October, the month in which Dad was expected to "check out," as he called it, he phoned to say he was flunking cancer. "The doctor showed me my blood markers and they're in a straight line, like test scores at school when you get the same grade over and over. Then they drop real sharp, like when you flunk a test. I'm flunking cancer!"

He went to the gym, swam laps, lifted weights, attended retiree luncheons, called on friends, and enjoyed Sunday night dinners at my brother's. He lent a hand to the neighbors, painted the foundation to the house, and replaced all the old light switches with new dimmer switches.

When his married grandson and his wife flew in for a visit, he asked if they'd like to go along on his walk the next morning. "Yes," they said.

"Good," he said. "See you at five."

They traipsed up and down hills for three miles in the Kansas City summer heat and humidity. They looped through a nearby business park and finished it off with thirty-three stairs up a steep embankment.

On rainy days I'd call to ask how he was and he'd say, "It's dreary and cold and wet here — a perfect day to be alive."

On sunny days I'd call and ask how he was and he'd say, "If I was any better, I'd explode!"

When it was time to renew the license tag on his car, he took the two-year option instead of the one.

Eventually, Dad began losing weight, fifty pounds in all, leaving him with little padding to cushion his bones. His one round of excruciating pain happened after he had been crawling around on the floor, while replacing a bathroom faucet. I flew in from Indianapolis. Dad opened the front door and said, "I'm so glad you came. I've wanted you to meet my doctor. He's something else."

My brother went to the appointment as well. The doctor's waiting room was buzzing with chatter about the 82-year-old man with pancreatic cancer who had been doing his own plumbing. My brother, who had been to previous appointments with my dad, leaned over and said, "Now when we get in there, there will be a lot of joshing and jawin', but none of it will be about cancer."

We were called back to an exam room, and after a few minutes the oncologist swung open the door and bellowed, "What were you doing plumbing?" To which my father responded, "What? You want I should stick to electrical work?" They joked and jawed and you'd never suspect the man on the table was facing death.

Soon after, hospice began checking on Dad weekly. "A nurse stopped by today," he said. "She's very nice, but she's rather heavy. I'm concerned about her." And he truly was.

Three days before Dad died, he went to the store to buy a birthday card for a friend and carried his next-door neighbor's recycling tub to her garage for her.

Dad died at home, surrounded by family. In the two years he lived under the cloud of cancer, there was never a trace of self-pity, only thanksgiving and gratitude for the gift of life and the extra time.

He was a father who taught his children well — both how to live and how to die.

Hub's 95 Theses

My father-in-law saw something that few people see: 95 candles on his birthday cake. He lived on his own in a big old farmhouse on a small acreage in Ohio.

If you asked him the secret to a long life, he would probably say, "What's that, honey?"

He was hard of hearing. Other than that, he had all his original parts and they were in good working order until he died at the age of 97 and three-quarters. He was proud of the three-quarters.

He mowed, cooked, drove, kept a daily journal for years, had quick reflexes, a phenomenal memory, and probably could have whipped that Ken Jennings, who had the long run on "Jeopardy!"

And he saved things. Plastic bags, empty margarine

tubs, license plates, ladders, chairs, old tools, empty bottles, newspapers, magazines, phone books. As the auctioneer said at the estate sale, "Ladies and gentlemen, three generations of the same family have lived in this house for more than a hundred years — and they never threw a single thing away!"

My father-in-law witnessed the evolution of automobiles, telephones, electric lights, airplanes, and air-conditioned combines. He outlasted flappers, gangsters, elevator attendants, streetcar conductors, moonshiners, segregation, and the days when a real person used to answer the phone.

He was married for nearly forty-nine years and a widower for almost a dozen more.

He was a life-long Lutheran, which is why on his ninety-fifth birthday we posted "Hub's 95 Theses," or the things we have learned to be true from knowing him.

In the interest of good health and a long life, I share the following few:

- Marry a good woman.

- Have children late in life; it keeps you young.

- Learn how to dance. Especially the polka.

- Own a convertible sometime in your life. Even if you don't buy it until you're 87.

- Let your hearing aids ring; it gives your kids and

grandkids something to talk about.

•Say "I love you" often.

•Tell interesting stories from the past, like remembering Armistice Day, seeing the first transcontinental flight fly overhead, and watching FDR's motorcade. It's a good way of teaching history and makes you an interesting dinner guest.

•Ignore the experts — eat lots of ham, sausage, bacon, and deli meats. Nitrates are the fountain of youth.

•Always shop with coupons.

•When you mow acreage, it's good to have one lawnmower and nine spares on hand.

•Groundhogs: if you can't kill 'em, outlive 'em.

•Train your grown kids to check in by phone every night at 9:45. Remind them not to go out after dark.

•Watch the Chicago news on WGN every night at ten; it makes wherever you live feel safe.

•Never leave home without checking The Weather Channel.

•Always lock The Club on your steering wheel.

•When the temperature is above seventy, unbutton

your shirt.

• When the temperature is above eighty, take it off.

• Read newspapers.

• A man can never have enough rolls of string, batteries, or mousetraps.

• Try fixing it with duct tape.

• Dress up for church — wear your white loafers.

• If you have grandkids over the age of twenty-seven who are single, remind them to get married.

• If it bends, creaks, or hurts, apply Icy Hot.

• Keep your water bill to the minimum.

• A bloody Mary a day keeps the doctor away.

• Wearing a pink shirt does not mean you are a metrosexual.

• Bolo ties are hip.

• Be friendly.

• Compliment the cook.

• Stay out of high-rise apartment buildings. They're unnatural.

• Always have a good joke ready to tell.

•It's OK to cry at weddings.

•Be generous to your kids and grandkids.

•Stock Werthers candy for your grandkids.

•Bargain for a senior discount at the gas pump.

•Save it, you never know when you'll need it.

•Never miss a high school reunion. Class of '28.

•Get one of those unlimited calling plans and stay in touch with friends and family.

•Thirty-three years of retirement from General Motors. GM — "Good to Me."

•Find a ball team (preferably the Reds) and follow them. It helps the loneliness.

Make My Obit a Good One

My father-in-law wrote out a lengthy list of information he wanted in his obituary on a piece of card stock and tucked it into his journal shortly before his death. At the top he wrote, "I hate stingy obits!" and underlined it four times with wavy blue lines. The family was instructed to make sure the obit was of good length and to pay no regard to the cost.

I love a well-written obit. If it's a great obit, I'll even save it.

There is a difference between a good obit and a great obit. A good obit makes you appreciate the life another human being has lived. A great obit makes you say, "Wow, I wish we could have done coffee."

One of my favorite obits is from woman named Ida

Davidoff. Davidoff was a well-known family therapist and expert on aging. Her obit in the *Los Angeles Times* read in part:

"When her four children grew up, she had a 'lovely depression' about her empty nest, then went back to college to earn a doctorate — at age fifty-seven — in marital and family counseling. When arthritis made it difficult to stoop over to tend her garden, she planted wildflowers in raised boxes. When her fingers got too stiff to play piano, she took singing lessons. Until recently she had baked her own bread, swum nude in her pool, and was 'always thinking ahead.'"

She was ninety-seven.

"She had no illusions about the vagaries of old age, describing her health as 'superb, considering' and telling one interviewer, 'If after sixty-five you wake up well without any pain or quake, you're dead.'"

"I live as if I'm going to live a long time. I'm planting bulbs, putting in shrubs that will take years to grow. Why deprive yourself of even an hour of beauty because you don't know how long you'll be around to enjoy it?"

She said there are four categories of life: "Babyhood, childhood, middle age," and "You look wonderful."

She was survived by a son, seven grandchildren, and nine great-grandchildren. I wish we could have done coffee.

You also know an obit is memorable if it makes the

news, like the obit written about a ninety-four-year-old great grandmother from Florida. It began fairly routine, then picked up spice.

Josie Anello, Tampa, was described as a "loving and faithful wife." The obit continued, "She is survived by her Son, 'A.J.', who loved and cared for her; Daughter 'Ninfa', who betrayed her trust, and Son, 'Peter', who broke her heart."

Anello's sixty-three-year-old son, A.J. Anello placed the obituary and accused his sixty-five-year-old sister, Ninfa Simpson, of stealing their mother's Social Security checks to go on vacations with her husband in Missouri and Alaska. Simpson denied the claims and said her brother was getting revenge with the obituary, but agreed with him that their brother Peter had been estranged from the family for twenty-five years.

Nothing is ever easy. Not even dying.

A friend's mother left a funeral file filled with instructions for the family to follow upon her death. My friend's mother had listed things she wanted in her obituary, the clothes she wanted to wear, or the "funeral outfit" that she had purchased several years before and still had the tags on. She also gave instructions on which rosaries she wanted in the casket, noting that one was from Ireland and the other from JFK's funeral mass. My friend has no idea how her mother would have gotten a rosary from JFK's funeral mass, but one does not question instructions in a funeral file.

Until it comes to music. The dearly deceased had specified two country western songs be played at her service. The woman never listened to country music, or particularly enjoyed country music, but knew that these two country songs were guaranteed to rip out mourners' hearts and leave them crying in their beer.

My friend drew the line at the tearjerker songs.

"Her friends are gone now. She wants an Aunt Mary funeral and it's simply not going to be an Aunt Mary funeral," my friend said.

Every family has at least one Aunt Mary funeral. It is the funeral of all funerals, well attended, lengthy line of mourners waiting to pay their respects, lots of hugging, crying and laughing, big floral arrangements, a wonderful eulogy, and a nice lunch afterward. The Aunt Mary funeral may be a fabulous funeral, but it comes with a catch. You have to die before all your friends.

I'd rather stick around and do coffee.

Cancel This

A funeral is like a wedding in reverse. With a wedding, you tend to a thousand details for months in advance and then have the big event. With a funeral, you have the big event and then tend to a thousand details in the months following.

It is amazing how many loose ends linger behind us after we depart. Some are funny, some are frustrating, and sometimes they are both — it all depends on your mental health.

After my mother died, I called AOL to cancel her internet service, a task that should have taken all of five minutes.

The customer service representative said I couldn't cancel the service because, and I quote, "Only the person who initiated the service can cancel the service."

I explained that the person who initiated the service was my mother and that she had died of a brain aneurysm.

To which the customer service representative replied that he was sorry, but the only way he could cancel service was if he received a letter requesting cancellation written by the person who had initiated the service.

"I told you she's deceased!" I snapped.

"The woman is not going to be writing any letters! She's not going to be writing letters to me, and she's certainly not going to be writing letters to you! What part of deceased don't you understand?"

Apparently, he didn't understand any part of it, as he apologized for not being able to help me and hung up the phone.

Right, have a nice day.

It took several more exasperating phone calls, a letter from me, a form to sign and date from AOL, and two months before the internet connection finally faded into cyberspace.

When my dad died, my brother called Sprint to cancel his cell phone.

The customer service rep explained that they didn't really like to cancel a cell phone contract (yes, well, and we really don't like it when a loved one dies, either) and suggested that someone in the family might enjoy the cell phone.

No, my brother said, just cancel the phone.

Then perhaps someone outside the family might enjoy the cell phone, the service rep said, continuing to push.

No, my brother said, just cancel the phone.

The customer rep said that to cancel the phone contract, he would need to see a death certificate.

My brother strongly disagreed and stated that the rep didn't need a death certificate, just cancel the phone. The rep insisted that he did need a death certificate, or Sprint would continue to bill for service.

"Tell you what," my brother said. "I'm not going to send you a death certificate, but what I will do is watch you try to get money from this guy."

It was a pretty good, "Can you hear me now?" moment.

I was on the Sprint website recently and saw a link to canceling a contract in the event of death. If they've made it easier, my brother deserves partial credit.

Socks and Bonds

Our parents are all gone, our fathers having died a little more than a year apart. A heavy door has swung shut with a resounding thud. Another generation has passed.

We now have become the ones who will answer the questions about home mortgages, stuffing turkeys, colicky babies, and buying tires.

The most daunting task that follows death is closing out houses.

So much stuff. You start sorting towels in one room and wind up grouping picture frames in another. If you don't have attention deficit disorder when you begin closing out a house, you will by the time you're finished.

Having handled a lot of stuff in the past few years, I've developed some ideas on what I want done with my stuff when I'm gone. The first rule when I die is this: Nobody goes through my underwear drawer.

I've done four underwear drawers now and there's no dignified way around it. I hereby dictate that upon my demise, my underwear drawer become a two-person project. One person holds open a trash bag and the second person empties the drawer.

This will eliminate any commentary about my socks, bras, and nighties. It should also preclude any and all discussion as to whether I actually thought that Spanx really did any good.

I won't want every drawer dumped wholesale. There's something therapeutic about going through your loved one's earthly belongings.

It's how you learn that your dad had fourteen pocket knives in his nightstand and liked pressed handkerchiefs. When you see that your mother used every spare dresser drawer for tablecloths and linens, it is affirmation that big parties are part of your heritage.

Bagging forty-three pairs of dress pants, including a blue seersucker and pink seersucker, etches into your memory that your father-in-law was a fashion risk-taker, even at ninety-seven.

Give my clothes to charity when I'm gone, but only the good stuff. We give a lot of garbage to non-profits. Why punish the poor?

After my clothes have been taken care of, I'd like family

members to move to the kitchen and take any dishes that make them smile. Maybe it's a serving bowl from a dinner that was a disaster or the pedestal plate that held triple-layer chocolate birthday cakes.

If there are still some nice things left, call my remaining cronies and tell them to come help themselves. If it's the same set of friends I have now, they'll need coffee and Danish.

As for the rest of the stuff, have a sale. But make it a respectable sale.

I want early bird specials from eight 'til ten. Honor the Bed Bath and Beyond coupons, Kohl's Cash, and the Macy's twenty percent off cards!

Set up a clearance area marked seventy-five percent off. Women will go wild!

5

WHO YOU CALLIN' GRANDMA?

A Grandma by Any Other Name

I never primed the pump for grandkids. Honestly, I really wasn't all that eager. In one sense, I looked at becoming a grandmother as one more giant nudge forward on that ever-shrinking timeline hurtling toward death. I've always had a knack for going dark.

So I wondered if when the time came, I would flip that switch. You know the one, the one where women suddenly become ga-ga over grandbabies. Would I become as crazy as other women when they became grandmothers? Would I get the grandma charm bracelet, the big banner sitting in the front yard congratulating myself on becoming a grandma? Would I lose all interest in books, ideas, and current events, opting instead to drone on and on about how adorable the baby is when she drools, how she rolls over, fills her diaper, smiles, burps, and ad infinitum?

Our first grandbaby arrived and the answer was yes. Unequivocally, yes.

When we visited the world's most beautiful grandbaby in the hospital, it was love at first sight. Head over heels love. Crazy throw-ourselves-in-front-of-a-speeding-train-for-her love.

We were absolutely enthralled with this beautiful baby girl. When my eyes finally adjusted to the golden glow she cast in the room, I couldn't help but notice she had one of those chunky plastic security tags on her leg.

My daughter-in-law explained that the security tag would set off an alarm if somebody — anybody — tried to remove the baby from the premises.

I smiled at the daughter-in-law, who glistened with the joy of motherhood.

I leaned to the baby and whispered in her ear that Grandma could slip that security tag right off her beautiful little leg and could give hospital security a run for their money.

I told her I had a vehicle ready to go in the parking lot.

I told her that I would buy Peanut Butter Captain Crunch, hire circus clowns, and let her stay up until midnight playing Wii, if she would come home with me.

I vaguely remember security guards dragging me from the Family Life Center over my vehement protests.

Who knew grandparenting could turn violent?

On the upside, it gave me a little more time to mull over the whole moniker thing.

People kept asking if I had chosen a name for myself. I didn't know grandmothers chose names. I thought you just waited to see what the kids hung on you and went with it.

A friend about to become a grandma said she would consent to being called Grandma only on the condition that others say, "You a grandma? No way! You're too young!"

I pondered being called Grandma and the alternate possibilities.

Oma was out, as it was my mother-in-law's given name and will always belong to her. Nana was good, but sounds like a woman who has her hair done and always matches her shoes with her purse. Those were standards too high for me to attain.

Granny was out. I didn't have a jalopy truck or a nephew named Jed.

I'm OK with Grandma. And hey, if you want to tell me I look too young to be a grandma, that's your business.

All that really matters is that the world's most beautiful baby makes a break for it and gets to Grandma's house real soon. I know she won't be eating solids for another twelve months, sweetie, but I've got the oven preheating and the cookie dough ready!

Times Two

Twins are not unfamiliar to my family. My mother came from a brood of seven children, which included younger sisters, Jean and Joyce, identical twins. She once used them for a 4-H project. She demonstrated a shampoo and set on one and the comb-out on the other.

Aunt Jean and Aunt Joyce have always carried a touch of ornery. I don't know if they were born ornery or being twins may have made them ornery, but they were two of the most fun aunts any kid could have.

It is impossible to imagine one without the other, because they were always "The Twins!" (to be said with excitement, as though a party is about to enter the room).

Because Jean and Joyce share a powerful bond, when they married and began having children, both of the twins named one of their daughters after the other twin.

Jean named a daughter Joyce, and Joyce named a daughter Jean. So Jean and Joyce are sisters and Jean has a Joyce and Joyce has a Jean.

Aunt Joyce had some health problems recently, but her daughter, Jean, was too overwhelmed to send out email updates, so Joyce, the daughter of Jean and niece of Joyce, sent out emails about Joyce and about taking her mother, Jean, to see Joyce and her daughter Jean.

In her emails, Joyce, the daughter of Jean, refers to Aunt Joyce, the sister of Jean, as Auntie J. Technically, Auntie J could be Aunt Jean or Aunt Joyce, so you really have to stop and think, was it Aunt Jean or Aunt Joyce who has been ill, and is it Aunt Joyce or Aunt Jean who is well?

When I last spoke on the phone with Aunt Jean, who has been well, thank you, I broke the news to her that our daughter and son-in-law were expecting twins. "Twin girls!" I chirped.

Aunt Jean's response was enthusiastic and immediate: "Oh, no!" she cried.

I had the impression Jean was speaking for Joyce as well, although I have yet to receive an email from Joyce, daughter of Jean, saying she has talked to Jean, daughter of Joyce, and confirmed that Aunt Joyce shares the sentiment of Aunt Jean.

And that is the story of Aunt Jean and Aunt Joyce and their daughters, Joyce and Jean.

Preemies

When our twin granddaughters arrived early, we were surprised that they were being called the big kids on the block. When you're closing in on four pounds in the neonatal intensive care unit, you pretty well qualify as middle linebackers.

Because the bruisers in soft pink and white sleepers are doing well and breathing on their own, they are being promoted to the unit known as The Village. Technically, this makes them Village People, although they have yet to jump up and sing "YMCA" and do the accompanying arm movements.

The two babies share an Isolette, a large clear plastic box with two holes on each side and one on the end so caretakers can tend to the babies without changing their air temperature. Moms and dads are encouraged to do all the hands-on care in The Village, changing diapers, comforting the babies, and taking the babies' temps at regular intervals.

The babies are swaddled separately amidst a tangle of wires for IV ports, heart, respiratory, and oxygen monitors. There is a ten-to-one blanket-to-baby ratio. Periodically, the Isolette begins looking like the morning after a slumber party. Blankets and bedding are piled high in wild disarray that says we stayed up all night, laughing, talking, drinking breast milk, and having a ball.

The babies are mirror images of one another, perfect in every detail, from their round little heads, to their almond shaped eyes, tiny noses, and delicate lips. And yet, like all preemies, they are not quite finished. They're on the scrawny side for linebackers. Their little legs lack meat and they would not be comfortable sitting on metal folding chairs.

There are three things preemies must learn to do when they are born. They must learn to breathe, feed, and maintain their own body temperature. This is what is happening in the Isolette. And one twin is doing this a little faster than the other.

But there is something else happening as well. The babies have been swaddled afresh and positioned side-by-side. There is a space of four inches between their little heads. One twin yawns and turns her head and the space between them narrows ever so slightly. Then the other one stretches her neck and the space narrows a little more. Slowly, almost imperceptibly, like watching a cloud slowly inch across the sky, the babies inch and wiggle until there is but a small sliver of space between them.

In an effort to help the twin who is not quite as adept at maintaining body temperature as the other one, a nurse swaddles them together in one blanket. Ah, heaven. They are now as close as they can be, not even a pinkie apart. The Isolette is covered with a heavy blanket and the babies are enveloped in shadows to simulate the environment in the womb.

A peek inside several minutes later reveals the one baby has laid her small pink hand on the other one's head as if to say, "Don't worry, I'll warm you."

And few minutes after that, they are holding hands.

Two preemies in an Isolette already have what nearly all mankind longs for — someone to share the journey with, someone who will give you a pat on the head, and someone to hold your hand.

Grandma Got Run Over by a Reindeer

I went to help with the twins when they were born. They weren't quite five pounds when they let them go home. Such scrawny little things. I broke out in a sweat every time I changed one of them. I was afraid I was going to break off an arm or a leg.

You know how everybody says, oh the baby is so pretty? It's one of the unwritten rules of the universe. Well, you don't say that with preemies. You say, "They'll grow, they'll grow."

They looked like baby birds. And then they grew a little and they looked like old men. It was like rocking Walter Mattheau to sleep in my arms.

I have always believed that dark circles and bags under the eyes of mothers and fathers of newborns are a new parent's badge of honor. But those same dark circles and bags under the eyes of a grandma look like a woman with a drinking problem aging before her time.

Sleep deprivation is never pretty. Consider the grandma, helping to care for newborn twins, who thought she accidently put a baby's sleeper in the Diaper Genie instead of the soiled diaper. The truly pathetic part is that the grandma shoved her hand into the Diaper Genie to check for the sleeper, when she could have simply looked in the laundry basket.

The next night, I changed both babies at three a.m. and a couple of hours later was summoned to the nursery by the new mother, who was giggling. Both babies' diapers were riding several miles south of their plumbing systems. To my credit, the diapers would have caught any fluids that leaked from the babies' knees.

"Tsk, tsk," I say to my daughter as we study the low-slung diapers. "Who would have thought those precious preemies would be dressing like thugs?"

The babies, who still side with their new mommy and daddy on everything because their brains are not yet developed enough to know that grandparents are their true allies, are again thrusting their arms into the air as though they have questions.

You don't have to be a baby whisperer to know what they are asking.

"Is Grandma sober?"

Yes, Grandma is sober; Grandma is just very tired.

"If Grandma is sober, why does she bump into the walls at night and stagger when she walks?"

Because Grandma is not used to sleeping in ninety-minute increments.

"Will we ever grow hair?"

Who knows."

What is the square root of eighty-one?"

"Nine. Now go to sleep."

Sleep deprivation is par for the course with newborns. When a clock says twelve, you ask yourself if that is midnight or noon. It is no longer a concern that you put your contact lens in the wrong eye and wonder if that is Tartar Control Crest or Handers Buttocks Ointment you just squeezed on your toothbrush.

I am grateful for our youngest, who calls once a day and shouts into the phone, "TODAY IS WEDNESDAY!" and then hangs up. In desperate times, little things mean a lot.

Sometimes during the day, the new-mommy daughter and I encourage one another with exchanges like the following:

"You look like someone blacked both your eyes."

"Thank you. Your hair looks like it was caught in the blender."

"I know. You look like you were marooned on a desert isle."

And on it goes, until one of the babies shoots an arm into the air with another question.

"Yes, dear?"

"What time does the party start tonight?"

The babies know good and well when the party starts — the minute the heads of all adults in the house hit the pillows and they think they have a shot at sleep.

Fast Trip, Even Faster Food

We are on a three-hour car ride to Chicago to see another new grandbaby (the fourth in less than two years, a prolific group are we). If you'd like to diagram this on a marker board, begin here: The husband is driving, the youngest daughter is in the passenger seat, the two twin grandbabies are strapped in the middle seats and their baby momma and myself are in the fold-up seats in the cargo area.

If you are diagramming, make the baby momma and myself itty bitty dots. Smaller. No, even smaller.

The fold-up seats in the back of an Explorer make airline seats that butt up against the restroom at the back of a plane look like La-Z-Boy recliners. Our knees are under our chins. This is remarkable, because we are both short.

Our legs, which were previously average length for short women, have now been folded and creased accordion-style and are the lengths of matchsticks.

This is one of those family trips that is a test of endurance. We've all had them. They are trips that are memorable, but should not, could not, and will not, ever be repeated.

Naturally, when traveling with small babies, the goal is to keep the car moving. As Isaac Newton discovered, a sleeping baby at rest is likely to remain a sleeping baby at rest. Or something like that.

In any case, the adult passengers are hungry, the driver could use some coffee, and the challenge is to grab some food without stopping the car or jostling the babies.

If we stop the car and slam car doors open and shut, there is a good chance the babies will wake. If we stop and the driver runs in for food, the front passenger must get out and rock the vehicle back and forth to make the babies think they are still in motion. The front passenger is unwilling.

Our best option is to use the drive-thru, drive as slowly as possible, order fast, pay fast, and come to a full stop only if absolutely necessary.

We have completed our mission. Now the challenge is how to get the food from the front seat to the far backseat. Everyone is wedged into their seat with baby gear, travel bags, handbags, and diaper bags. I am assessing the situation, when the front passenger softly says, "Catch!" A hamburger hurls through the dark in my direction.

That's right, a full-beef patty on bun with ketchup, mustard, pickle, and onion sails into the far backseat.

"What are you thinking?" I whisper shout.

"What's the matter? You have a hamburger, don't you?" she whisper shouts back.

"Yes, but it came with a wind shear and the pickle left skid marks on my right forearm."

She says I am exaggerating and, besides, the burger was still wrapped.

"Partially wrapped," I correct. "And only because I am a good catch."

One of the babies starts to stir, no doubt startled by the wind shear created by the flying burger.

If we ever lose our minds and make another trip like this, we will certainly not be ordering anything from the drive-through with shredded lettuce, tomato slices or onion rings.

Come to think of it, fries are out, too.

Tacos would be unthinkable.

The Smudgers Strike Again

I've always considered flowers or candles appropriate hostess gifts but, as a grandmother, I often find myself thinking it may be time to add Windex to the list.

The entire family descended on my brother and sister-in-law's place for my nephew's wedding. Our mob included the four grandbabies, one three-year-old and three under the age of two.

My brother and his wife do not yet have grandbabies. You can tell this by the big beautiful windows in their sun-room, the sparkling glass top coffee table, the glass top end table, and the full-view glass doors.

You can also tell because the trash can under the sink does not smell like diapers.

The grandbabies could tell all this, too, which is why

they promptly initiated the place. After twenty minutes of the shy, coy routine, they cut loose in the sunroom. They stampeded around the room, patting their little hands on every window. One cut from the herd, shot to an end table and shook a Good Housekeeping without mercy. Just as an adult salvaged the magazine, another tot dove for a hard-back book on North American birds.

The bird book was rescued and they all congregated at the coffee table. They circled the table slowly, dragging their fat little hands on the glass top as they walked around and around. For an extra something special, one saw her reflection in the glass, leaned down and gave herself a big wet kiss.

The three-year-old began removing cushions from the wicker settee and was joined by a cousin. The cushions were ordered back in place as a large potted plant began quivering in the corner. The youngest was wedged in the corner, wielding a death grip on the pot, shaking it violently.

My brother corralled the four of them on the sofa and said, "Smudgers, that's what they are. Every last one of them. Smudgers!"

"Outside!" someone yelled. The smudgers wiggled to the floor and cut for the door leading to the deck. More space to run! They circled another nephew, who is vision impaired, sitting at an outdoor table. Then they circled his German Shepherd guide dog. (We show no mercy in this family.) And then they abruptly reversed course. Had they not reversed course, they may have missed it — a second full-view glass door leading from the deck. Not one, but *two* doors they could rub their little hands on and smash their little faces against.

One of the twins grunted to go inside and the door opened. She was on the inside and her twin was outside. It was the royal double smudge! They each smeared opposite sides of the glass.

"To the yard!" someone yelled. They stampeded into the green space. It was the old divide and conquer. One bee-lined to splash in a kiddie pool where a Golden Retriever lounged in the heat. The others dashed to the chicken coop. They circled the chicken pen, alternately scaring the Rhode Island Reds and being scared by them.

The short flash mob bolted back to the house to once again smudge all the windows, doors, and glass table tops. This time, they had wet hands, so it was an even better smudge.

When it was time to go, they said they were sorry to see us leave. Funny though, it looked like they were smiling.

Of course, it was hard to see, they were standing in the window.

After the Last Pine Needle Has Fallen

Cleanup after the holidays with adult children and grandchildren is like the aftermath of a natural disaster without aid from the Red Cross, sandbags, or a hoard of volunteers.

We have washed sheets on every bed and laundered every towel. We have picked red and green sprinkles from sugar cookies out of the microwave and made a list of the missing Scrabble tiles. We have pitched fossilized fudge, stale chips, and flat soda, and are still picking stray pine needles and glitter off tablecloths and turtlenecks.

Slowly, very slowly, the house is returning to order one square foot at a time. Three pack 'n plays are folded up and returned to the closet. Sheets are stripped from the crib, one booster seat is wiped down, two strap-in-the-chair high chairs are cleaned, and a collapsible high chair is sponged off and returned to a neighbor.

Beyond that, much of the cleanup resembles a search and rescue mission. So far, one light green pacifier on a clip chain has been found, a baby bottle on a dining room chair, infant Tylenol, one pair of unclaimed paisley rain boots in a bathroom, and a plastic dinosaur hiding beneath the sofa.

The dryer coughs up two bibs, and an unfamiliar sock and a burp cloth are found quivering behind a wingback chair. "It's OK to come out now; they've all gone home!"

Frosty is melting outside and all that's left of the kiddie snow slide is a clump of snow. Who needs photographs to preserve fun-in-the-snow memories when you have the entire family's boot prints outlined on your kitchen floor?

And fingerprints. They're on the windows, doors, refrigerator, stove, and dishwasher, sometimes with food clinging to them, sometimes not. It seems harsh to wipe them all away, so we left a few for memories.

The house is recovering from an after-the-party look without the empty beer cans. What a party it was.

Hard to believe that just a week ago the front hall resembled a hitching post to a saloon, only instead of horses lined up, there were car seats and strollers. "Move over there, Trigger, we've got a double stroller comin' through."

But now the car seats and strollers are gone. We've taken down the tree, gathered the decorations, and packed them away until next year. The final plastic storage tub is hoisted onto a shelf in the garage as a stray snow globe is discovered in a bedroom. It's Mary and Joseph and the baby Jesus in a manger in a flurry of neon snow. It's coming back to me now. Someone was winding up "The First Noel" over and over in the middle of the night, trying to get a baby to sleep.

We can sleep like a baby now. It is quiet. Very quiet.

They've all gone back to their respective corners.

We'll haul the trash bags out to the curb, run the vacuum, and sweep away the crumbs, but not the memories.

Is that a tear in my eye, the husband asks?

"A tear of joy," I say. "We now have a clean house to ourselves, full possession of the remote, and three-hundred sixty-five days before we do it all again."

Am I There Yet?

There comes a time in every woman's life when she wakes up, staggers from the bed to the bathroom with one knee clicking, and looks in the mirror. She winces at a sharp pain in her left shoulder, gazes at the wild hair from a restless night of no sleep, the deepening crinkles that defy the night cream guaranteed to defy age, and the blotchy skin due in part to a thick slice of Kentucky Derby pie the day before.

The bags under the eyes are a gift from her mother's side. The fine lines around the mouth that make her look like she's a three-pack-a-day smoker have come from her father.

She takes a good, long, hard look and asks herself, "Have I reached the point of diminishing returns?"

In business, the point of diminishing returns means seeing a smaller rise in product output despite an increase in the production process input. It's when the additional fertilizer on the crops no longer guarantees a fuller ear of corn.

Am I there yet? Have I reached that place where the fertilizer no longer gives a fuller ear of corn? Am I at the point of diminishing returns?

Am I at that point where the kids are grown and I've worked myself out of a job?

Am I at the point where I don't recognize the names of the Thirty-Something celebs having birthdays and don't care, so I am now culturally irrelevant?

Am I at the point where I think twice about reaching out to the new neighbor or taking a meal to new mothers because maybe they'd rather chat with someone their own age?

Am I at that point where I believe the lie that age means you're not valuable anymore?

I meet interesting people at some of the groups I address. Frankly, the older ones tend to be the most interesting ones. They're the ones with the better stories and longer histories.

I was invited to speak to a group of women gathered to raise money for women in their community. The head table began buzzing because the woman who was to be recognized as the Woman of the Year had not yet arrived.

The woman they were waiting for was ninety.

Doris has refused to come to the event with either of her daughters because she prefers to drive herself.

"Who knows, maybe she stopped off at Wal-Mart on her way for a bag of cat food," one of her daughters said.

"Maybe she's working on the gallery opening tonight," someone offered.

Doris had taught art at the high school, founded the fine arts council in town and "brought culture to the county," as they called it. When she retired from teaching, she painted the history of the town on a wall mural in the high school, working on 15-foot scaffolding.

Time passed, the room filled, the emcee made some announcements, and still no Doris.

"Does she have a cell phone?" someone asked.

"Yes, but she's not answering."

The festive atmosphere began to mute. Anxious eyes fixed on the door.

"Maybe she's having trouble finding parking," someone said.

More quiet. More waiting. Finally. Doris breezes in through a side door.

She takes her seat and puts her pocketbook on the floor. Others look at her expectantly, waiting for an explanation. She says, "My friend Joe died Wednesday." A collective gasp circles the table as the others clearly do not have the same pipeline Doris does, and have not heard about Joe.

"I got a call Wednesday night," she says. "So I made some chicken salad last night, took it over to the house this morning, and sat awhile."

Doris hadn't bought the business about kicking back and staring at the wall when you pass a certain age. She was still on the go. Good luck catching her.

Hard work, a life well-lived, and giving to others along the way is that quiet recipe for greatness so often overlooked.

Are you there yet? Have you reached the point of diminishing returns?

Your outside package may change over time, but your core remains the same. You will always be someone's wife, mother, grandmother, sister, daughter or friend. You will always be someone's favorite aunt, special neighbor, prayer warrior, listening ear, or bright spot in the day.

Are you there yet? Have you reached the point of diminishing returns?

Never.

You will always have something to contribute.